A-Z GUILDFORD

G000298382

Key to Map Pages	Back Cover
Map Pages	2-37

Large S...

Index to
selected...

REFERENCE

Motorway	M25	Car Park (selected)	P
A Road	A332	Church or Chapel	†
B Road	B2234	Cycleway (selected)	
Dual Carriageway		Fire Station	■
One-way Street Traffic flow on A roads is also indicated by a heavy line on the drivers' left.	→	Hospital	H
Road Under Construction Opening dates are correct at the time of publication.		House Numbers (A & B Roads only)	2 33
Proposed Road		Information Centre	i
Restricted Access		National Grid Reference	525
Pedestrianized Road		Park & Ride	Onslow P+R
Residential Walkway		Police Station	▲
Track		Post Office	★
Footpath		**Safety Camera with Speed Limit** Fixed cameras and long term road works cameras. Symbols do not indicate camera direction.	30
Railway	Station / Level Crossing / Tunnel	**Toilet:** without facilities for the Disabled with facilities for the Disabled	▽ ▽
Built-up Area	WARD ST	Viewpoint	⁂
Local Authority Boundary	—··—··—	Educational Establishment	▢
Posttown Boundary		Hospital or Healthcare Building	▢
Postcode Boundary (within Posttown)	—·—·—	Industrial Building	▢
		Leisure or Recreational Facility	▢
		Place of Interest	▢
Map Continuation 22	Large Scale Town Centre 38	Public Building	▢
		Shopping Centre or Market	▢
		Other Selected Buildings	▢

SCALE

Map Pages 2-37   1:19,000

0   ¼   ½ Mile
0   250   500   750 Metres
3.33 inches (8.47cm) to 1 mile   5.26cm to 1 km

Map Page 38   1:9,500

0   ⅛   ¼ Mile
0   100   200   300 Metres
6.67 inches (16.94 cm) to 1 mile   10.53 cm to 1 km

A-Z AZ AtoZ
registered trade marks of
Geographers' A-Z Map Company Ltd

www./az.co.uk

EDITION 4 2016
Copyright © Geographers' A-Z Map Co. Ltd.
Telephone: 01732 781000 (Enquiries & Trade Sales)
01732 783422 (Retail Sales)
© Crown copyright and database rights 2015 OS 100017302.
Safety camera information supplied by www.PocketGPSWorld.com.
Speed Camera Location Database Copyright 2015 © PocketGPSWorld.com

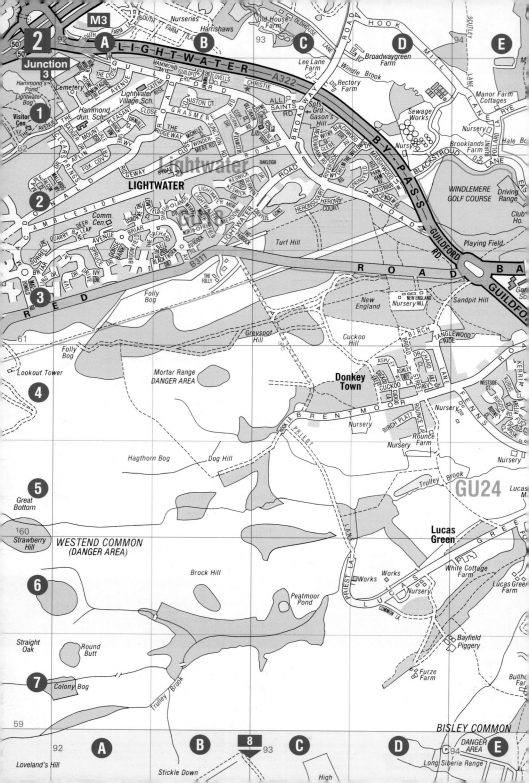

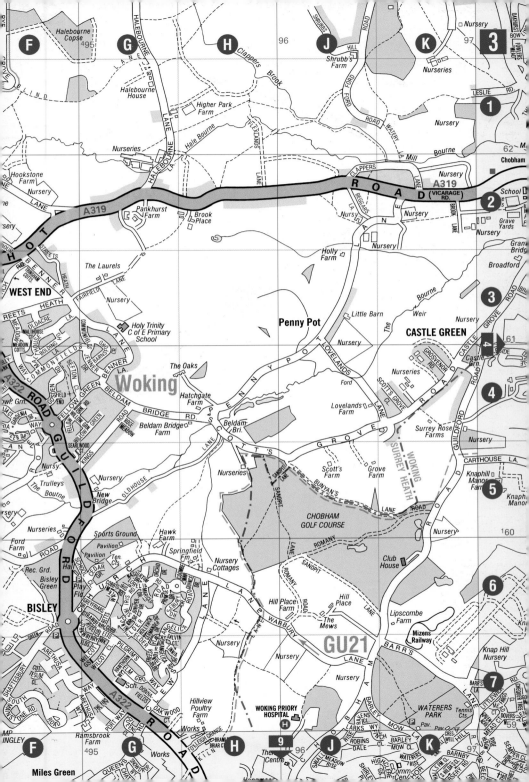

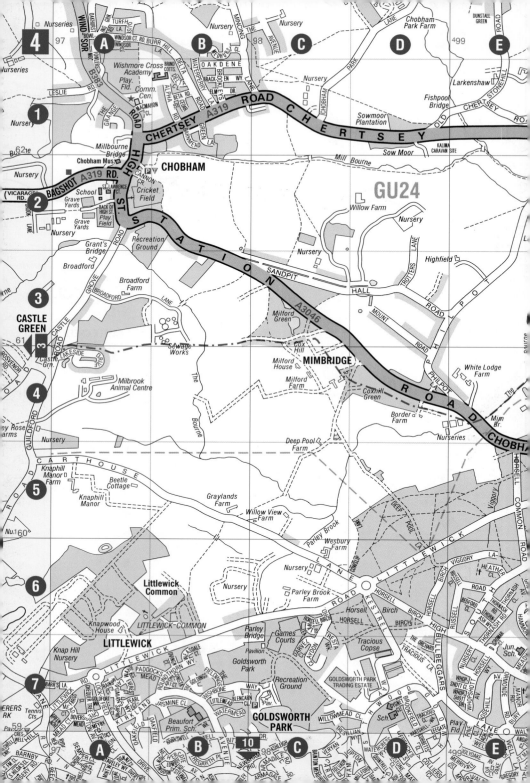

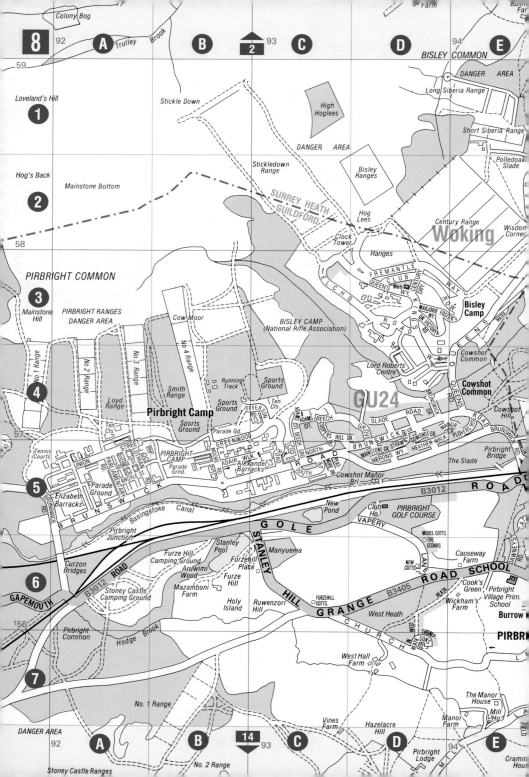

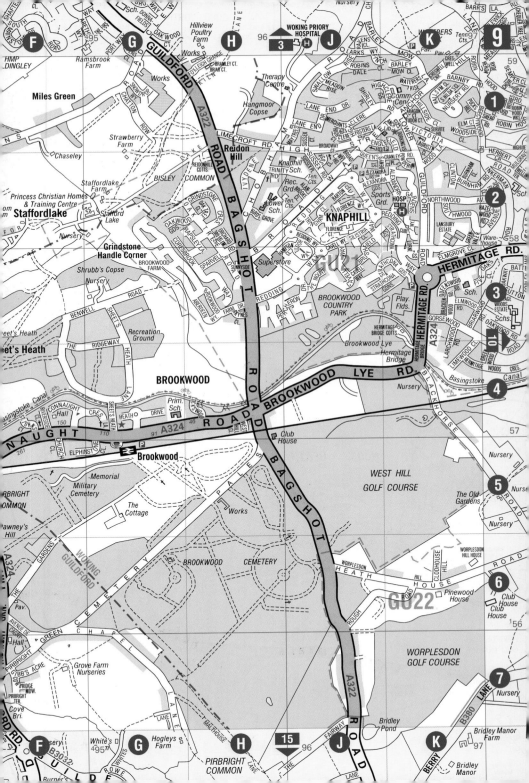

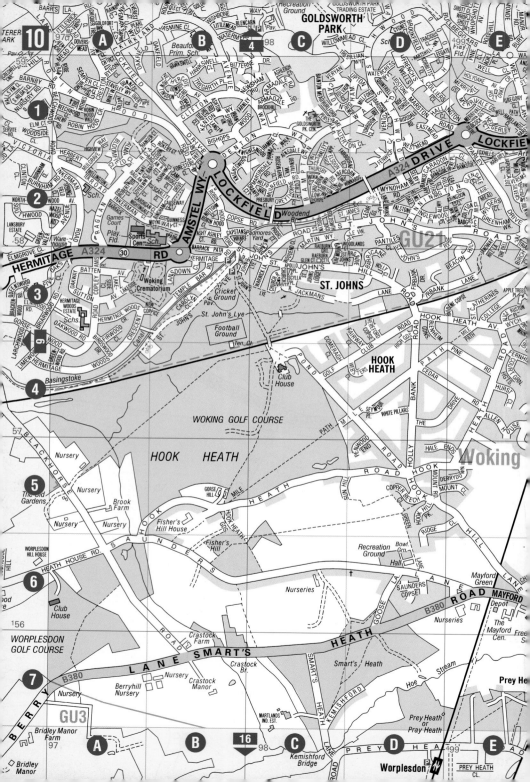

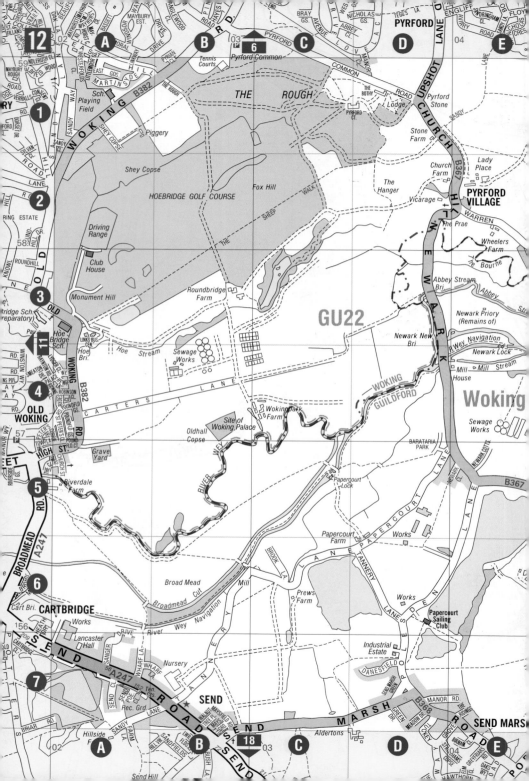

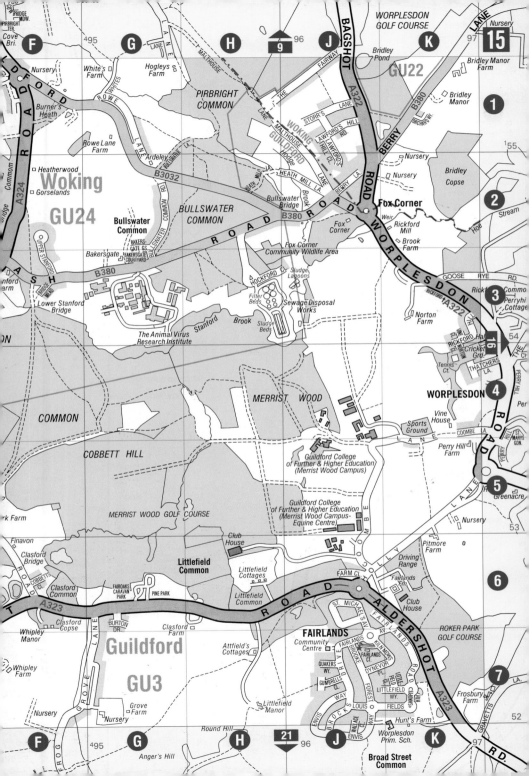

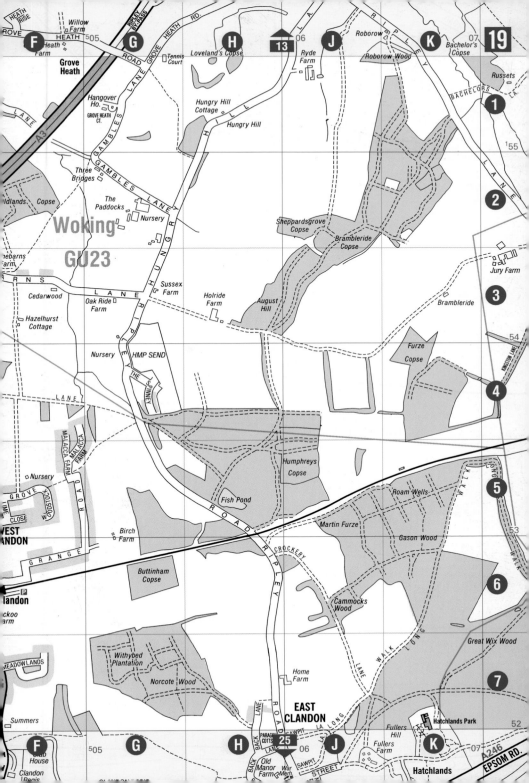

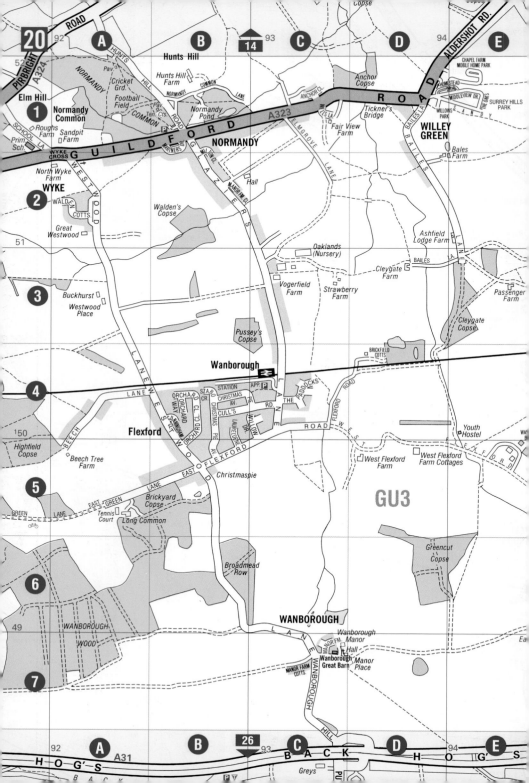

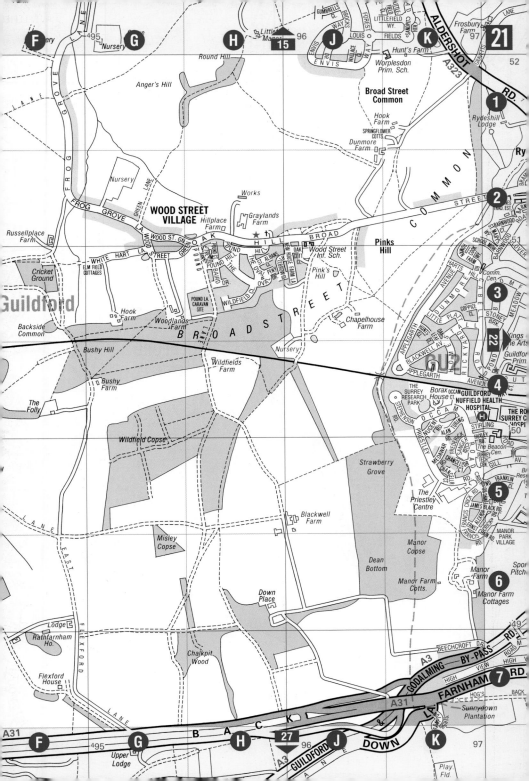

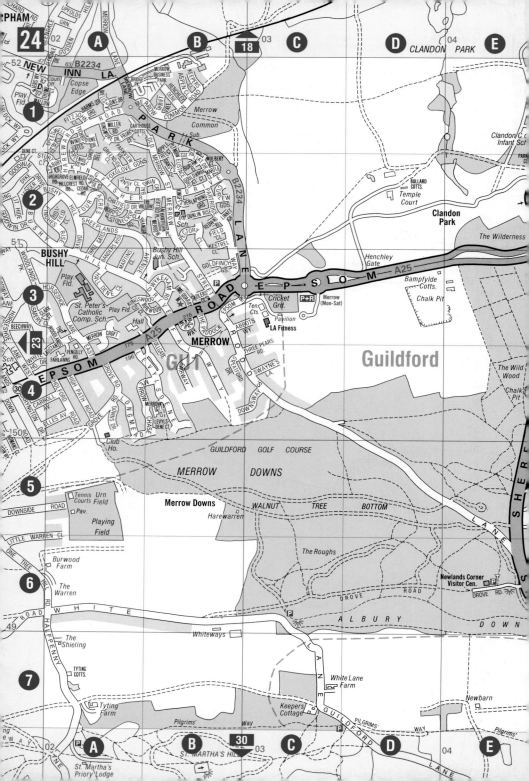

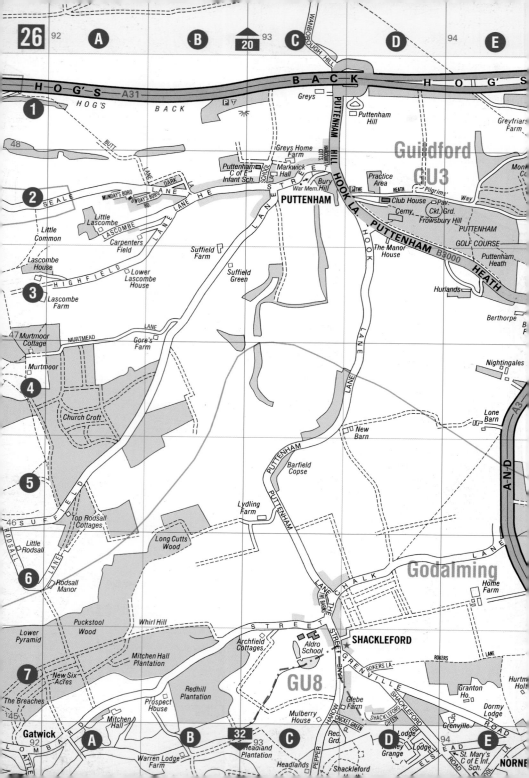

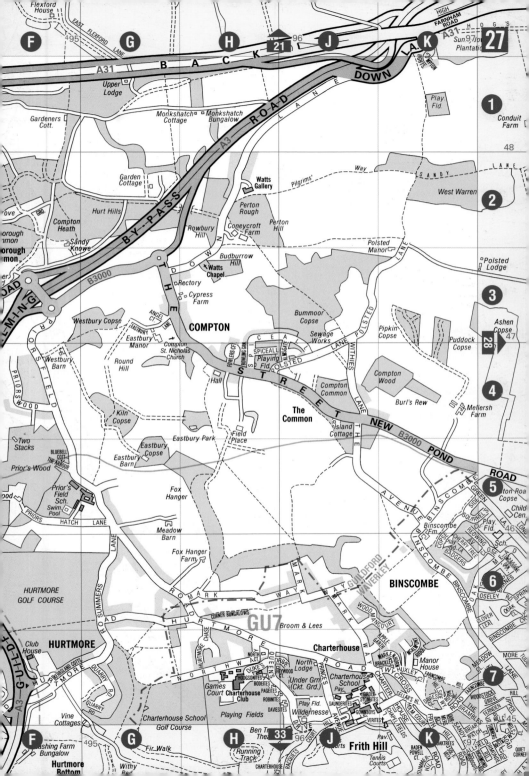

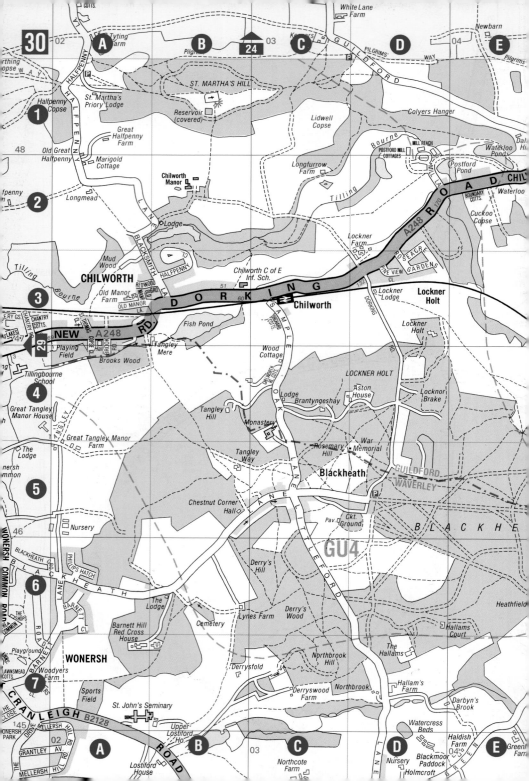

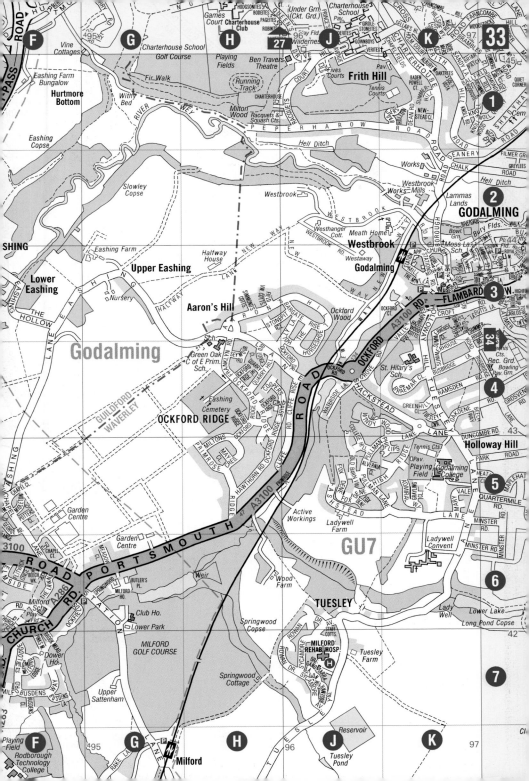

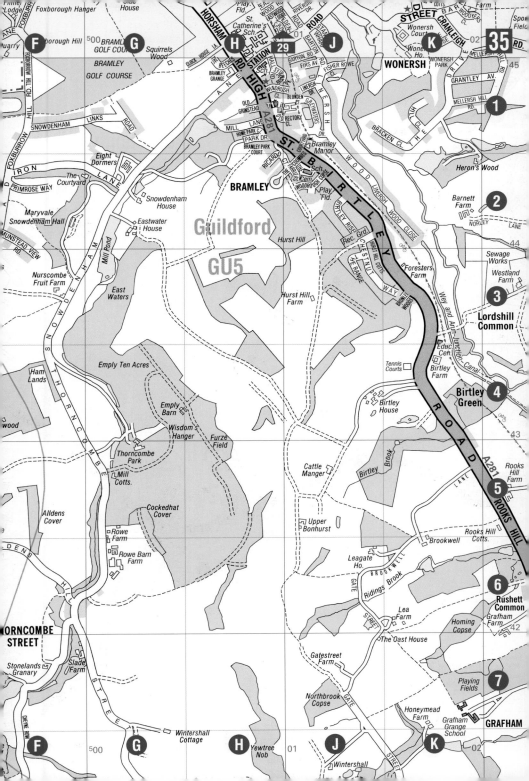

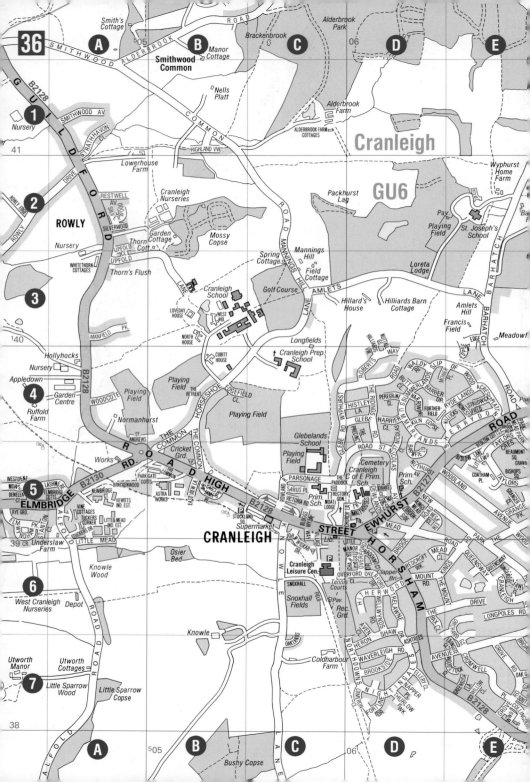

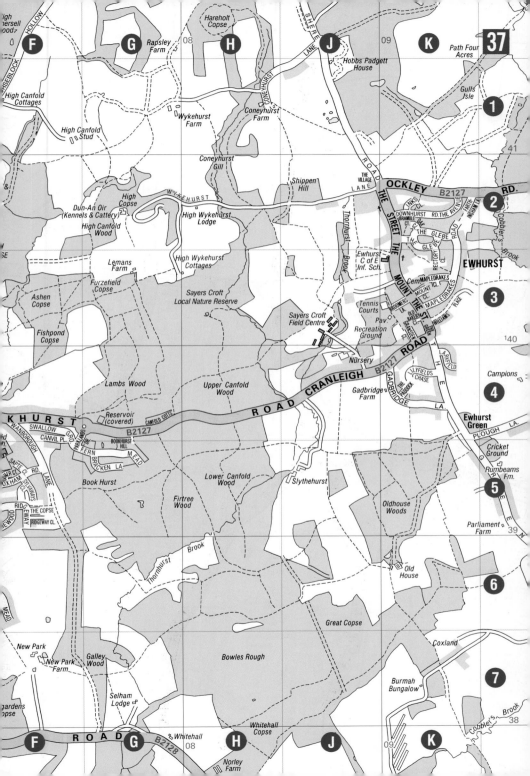

INDEX

Including Streets, Places & Areas, Hospitals & Hospices, Industrial Estates,
Selected Flats & Walkways, Stations and Selected Places of Interest.

HOW TO USE THIS INDEX

1. Each street name is followed by its Postcode District, then by its Locality abbreviation(s) and then by its map reference;
   e.g. **Aaron's Hill** GU7: G'mng . . . .3H *33* is in the GU7 Postcode District and the Godalming Locality and is to be found in square 3H on page **33**.
   The page number is shown in bold type.

2. A strict alphabetical order is followed in which Av., Rd., St., etc. (though abbreviated) are read in full and as part of the street name;
   e.g. **Brookmead Cl.** appears after **Brook Mead** but before **Brook Rd.**

3. Streets and a selection of flats and walkways that cannot be shown on the mapping, appear in the index with the thoroughfare to which they are
   connected shown in brackets; e.g. **Abbeyfield** GU1: Guild . . . .5H *23* (off Lwr. Edgeborough Rd.)

4. Addresses that are in more than one part are referred to as not continuous.

5. Places and areas are shown in the index in BLUE TYPE and the map reference is to the actual map square in which the town centre or area is located and not
   to the place name shown on the map; e.g. BISLEY CAMP 3D 8

6. An example of a selected place of interest is Chobham Mus. 2A 4

7. Example of stations are:
   Brookwood Station (Rail) . . . .5G 9; Artington (Park & Ride) . . . .2E 28; Guildford Bus Station 4B 38 (5E 22)

8. An example of a Hospital, Hospice or selected Healthcare facility is ALPHA HOSPITAL, WOKING 2K 9

9. Map references for entries that appear on large scale page **38** are shown first, with small scale map references shown in brackets;
   e.g. **Abbot Rd.** GU1: Guild 6D **38** (6F *23*)

GENERAL ABBREVIATIONS

All. : Alley	**Ct.** : Court	**Info.** : Information	**Rd.** : Road
App. : Approach	**Cres.** : Crescent	**La.** : Lane	**Shop.** : Shopping
Av. : Avenue	**Cft.** : Croft	**Lit.** : Little	**Sth.** : South
Bri. : Bridge	**Dr.** : Drive	**Lwr.** : Lower	**Sq.** : Square
Bldgs. : Buildings	**E.** : East	**Mnr.** : Manor	**St.** : Street
Bungs. : Bungalows	**Est.** : Estate	**Mdw.** : Meadow	**Ter.** : Terrace
Bus. : Business	**Fld.** : Field	**Mdws.** : Meadows	**Twr.** : Tower
Cvn. : Caravan	**Flds.** : Fields	**M.** : Mews	**Trad.** : Trading
Cen. : Centre	**Gdn.** : Garden	**Mt.** : Mount	**Up.** : Upper
Chyd. : Churchyard	**Gdns.** : Gardens	**Mus.** : Museum	**Va.** : Vale
Circ. : Circle	**Ga.** : Gate	**Nth.** : North	**Vw.** : View
Cir. : Circus	**Gt.** : Great	**Pde.** : Parade	**Vs.** : Villas
Cl. : Close	**Grn.** : Green	**Pk.** : Park	**Vis.** : Visitors
Comn. : Common	**Gro.** : Grove	**Pas.** : Passage	**Wlk.** : Walk
Cnr. : Corner	**Hgts.** : Heights	**Pl.** : Place	**W.** : West
Cott. : Cottage	**Ho.** : House	**Quad.** : Quadrant	**Yd.** : Yard
Cotts. : Cottages	**Ind.** : Industrial	**Ri.** : Rise	

LOCALITY ABBREVIATIONS

Albury: GU5 . . . . .Alb	East Clandon: GU4 . . . . . . .E Clan	Ockham: GU23 . . . . .Ock	Thursley: GU8 . . . . .Thur
Alfold: GU6 . . . . .Alf	Elstead: GU8 . . . . .Els	Ottershaw: KT16 . . . . .Ott	Wanborough: GU3 . . . . .Wanb
Artington: GU3,GU7 . . . . . . .Art	Enton Green: GU8 . . . . . . .Ent G	Peasmarsh: GU3,GU7 . . . .Peasm	West Byfleet: KT14 . . . . . . .W Byf
Bisley: GU24 . . . . .Bisl	Ewhurst: GU6 . . . . .Ewh	Peper Harow: GU8 . . . . . . .P Har	West Clandon: GU4 . . . . . . .W Cla
Blackheath: GU4 . . . . .Blckh	Flexford: GU3 . . . . .Flex	Pirbright: GU24 . . . . .Pirb	West End: GU24 . . . . .W End
Bramley: GU5 . . . . .Bram	Godalming: GU7-8 . . . . . . .G'mng	Puttenham: GU3 . . . . .Putt	West Horsley: KT24 . . . . . . .W Hor
Brook: GU8 . . . . .Brook	Gomshall: GU5 . . . . .Goms	Pyrford: GU22 . . . . .Pyr	Weybridge: KT13 . . . . .Weyb
Brookwood: GU21,GU24 . . .Brkwd	Guildford: GU1-5 . . . . .Guild	Ripley: GU23 . . . . .Rip	Windlesham: GU20 . . . . . .W'sham
Burpham: GU1,GU4 . . . . . .Burp	Hambledon: GU8 . . . . .H'don	Rudgwick: GU6 . . . . .Rudg	Wisley: GU23 . . . . .Wis
Busbridge: GU7-8 . . . . .Bus	Hurtmore: GU7 . . . . .Hurt	Seale: GU10 . . . . .Seale	Witley: GU8 . . . . .Wit
Byfleet: KT14 . . . . .Byfl	Jacobs Well: GU4 . . . . . . .Jac W	Send: GU23 . . . . .Send	Woking: GU21-22,GU24 . . . .Wok
Chertsey: KT16 . . . . .Chert	Knaphill: GU21 . . . . .Knap	Shackleford: GU8 . . . . . . .Shack	Wonersh: GU5 . . . . .Wone
Chobham: GU24 . . . . .Chob	Lightwater: GU18-19 . . . . .Light	Shalford: GU4 . . . . .Shalf	Woodham: KT15 . . . . .Wdhm
Compton: GU3 . . . . .Comp	Milford: GU8 . . . . .Mil	Shamley Green: GU5 . . . . .Sha G	Wood Street Village: GU3 . . .Woo V
Cranleigh: GU6 . . . . .Cranl	New Haw: KT15 . . . . .New H	Shere: GU5 . . . . .Shere	Wormley: GU8 . . . . .Worm
Eashing: GU7 . . . . .Eash	Normandy: GU3 . . . . .Norm	Sutton Green: GU4 . . . . . . .Sut G	Worplesdon: GU3 . . . . .Worp

A

	Acacia Cl. KT15: Wdhm 1D *6*	Albury Pk. GU5: Alb 2J *31*	Allen Ho. Pk. GU22: Wok 4E *10*
	Acacia Dr. KT15: Wdhm 1D *6*	Albury Rd. GU1: Guild 5H *23*	Allingham Ct. GU7: G'mng 7B *28*
AARON'S HILL 3H *33*	Acacia Rd. GU1: Guild . . .1C **38** (4F *23*)	Alcorn Cl. GU24: Chob 2B *34*	Alloway Ct. KT14 . . . . .2D *10*
Aaron's Hill GU7: G'mng 3H *33*	Access Bus. Pk. KT14: Byfl 2H *7*	Alderbrook Farm Cotts.	All Saints Rd. GU18: Light 1C *2*
Abbey Cl. GU22: Pyr 7C *6*	Acer Dr. GU24: W End 4F *3*	GU6: Cranl 1C *36*	Alma Cl. GU21: Knap 1A *10*
Abbey Cl. GU21: Wok 1E *10*	Achilles Pl. GU21: Wok 1E *10*	Alderbrook Rd. GU6: Cranl . . .1A *36*	Almond Av. GU22: Wok 5F *11*
Abbeyfield GU1: Guild 5H *23*	Acorn Gro. GU22: Wok 5G *11*	Alders, The KT14: W Byf 3G *7*	Almond Cl. GU1: Guild 1F *23*
(off Lwr. Edgeborough Rd.)	Acres Platt GU6: Cranl 4E *36*	Aldersey Rd. GU1: Guild 4H *23*	Almsgate GU3: Comp 4J *27*
Abbey Mill Bus. Pk. GU7: Eash . . .3E *32*	Adair Wlk. GU24: Brkwd 5B *8*	Aldershot Rd. GU2: Guild 6K *15*	ALPHA HOSPITAL, WOKING 2K *9*
Abbey Rd. GU21: Wok 1E *10*	Adams Cft. GU24: Brkwd 4C *8*	GU3: Guild, Norm, Worp . . .7E *14*	Alpha Rd. GU22: Wok 7K *5*
Abbot Cl. KT14: Byfl 1H *7*	Addison Ct. GU1: Guild 6H *23*	GU24: Chob 1B *4*	Alresford Rd. GU2: Guild 5C *22*
Abbot Rd. GU1: Guild . . .6D **38** (6F *23*)	Addison Rd. GU1: Guild 6G *23*	Alexander Fleming Rd.	Alterton Cl. GU21: Wok 1C *10*
	GU21: Wok 1H *11*	GU2: Guild 5K *21*	Alvernia Cl. GU7: G'mng 5J *33*
Abbot's Cl. GU2: Guild 7A *22*	Admirals Ct. GU1: Guild 3K *23*	Alexandra Gdns. GU21: Knap . . .2J *9*	Alwyne Ct. GU21: Wok 7G *5*
Abbotsford Cl. GU22: Wok 1J *11*	Admiral's Rd. GU24: Pirb 3A *14*	Alexandra Pl. GU1: Guild 6H *23*	Ambassadors Cinema
Abbots Hospital GU1: Guild . . .4D **38**	Admiral Way GU7: G'mng 5K *33*	Alexandra Ter.	Woking 1G *11*
Abbots Way GU1: Guild 3B *24*	Agraria Rd. GU2: Guild 5D *22*	GU1: Guild 3E **38** (5G *23*)	(off Victoria Way)
ABBOTSWOOD 2H *23*	Ainsdale Way GU21: Wok 2C *10*	Alford Cl. GU4: Burp 1H *23*	Amberley Cl. GU23: Send 2D *18*
Abbotswood GU1: Guild 2H *23*	Alanbrooke Cl. GU21: Knap 2J *9*	Alford Rd. GU4: Burp 1H *23*	Amberley Dr. KT15: Wdhm 1D *6*
Abbotswood Cl. GU1: Guild . . .1H *23*	Alan Turing Rd. GU2: Guild . . .4K *21*	Alice Ruston Pl. GU22: Wok 3E *10*	Amberley La. GU8: Mil 6E *32*
Abelia Cl. GU24: W End 4E *2*	Albert Dr. GU21: Wok 6K *5*	Alison Cl. GU21: Wok 6G *5*	Amberley Rd. GU8: Mil 5E *32*
Abercorn Way GU21: Wok 2C *10*	Albion Ho. GU21: Wok 1H *11*	Allden Cotts. GU7: G'mng 3H *33*	Amberside Cl. GU21: Wok 2C *34*
Aberdeen Way GU21: Knap 3K *9*	**ALBURY** 2F *31*	(off Aaron's Hill)	Ambleside Cl. GU18: Light 2A *2*
Abingdon Cl. GU21: Wok 2E *10*	**ALBURY HEATH** 4J *31*	Alldens Hill GU5: Bram 6F *35*	Ambleside Rd. GU18: Light 1G *5*
Abingdon Cl. GU22: Wok 2H *23*	Albury Ho. GU1: Guild 6H *23*	GU8: Bus 6F *35*	Amis Av. KT15: New H 1E *6*
Abinger Way GU4: Burp 6K *17*	Albury M. GU7: G'mng 1K *33*	Alldens La. GU8: Bus 5D *34*	Amis Rd. GU21: Wok 3A *10*
Acacia Av. GU22: Wok 4F *11*			

Amlets La. GU6: Cranl 3C 36
Amstel Way GU21: Wok 2B 10
Anchor Cl. GU3: Norm 1C 20
Anchor Cres. GU21: Knap 1K 9
Anchor Hill GU21: Knap 1K 9
Anderson Cl. GU2: Guild 7D 16
Angel Cl. GU3: Comp 3G 27
GU7: G'mng 3K 33
Angel Ga. GU2: Guild 4C 38 (5F 23)
Angelica Rd. GU2: Guild 7C 16
GU24: Bisl 6G 3
Annandale Rd. GU2: Guild 6D 22
ANNINGSLEY PARK 1A 6
Anningsley Pk. KT16: Ott 1K 5
Anston Ct. GU2: Guild 4A 22
ANTHONYS 3J 5
Apers Av. GU22: Wok 5H 11
Apex Ct. KT14: W Byf 3F 7
Aplin Way GU18: Light 2A 2
Apollo Pl. GU3: Norm 3C 10
Applegarth GU7: G'mng 7K 27
Applegarth Av. GU2: Guild 4K 21
Appletree Cl. GU7: Bus 5B 34
Appletree Ct. GU4: Guild 1B 24
Apple Trees Pl. GU22: Wok 3E 10
Aprilwood Cl. KT15: Wdhm 2D 6
Aragon Ct. GU21: Knap 1K 9
Aragon Wlk. KT14: Byfl 4K 7
Aragorn Ct. GU2: Guild 2D 22
Aram Ct. GU22: Wok 6A 6
Arbour, The GU7: Hurt 5F 27
Ardmore Cl. GU2: Guild 2D 22
Ardmore Ho. GU2: Guild 2D 22
Ardmore Way GU2: Guild 2D 22
Arethusa Way GU24: Bisl 7F 3
Argyle St. GU24: Brkwd 5A 8
Armadale Rd. GU21: Wok 1C 10
Arnold Rd. GU2: Wok 6K 5
Arreton Mead GU21: Wok 5H 5
Arthur's Bri. Rd. GU21: Wok 1E 10
Arthur's Bri. Wharf GU21: Wok 1F 11
Artillery Rd. GU1: Guild 3C 38 (5F 23)
Artillery Ter. GU1: Guild 2C 38 (4F 23)
ARTINGTON 2E 28
Artington
(Park & Ride) 2E 28
Artington Wlk.
GU2: Guild 7B 38 (7E 22)
Arundel Ho. GU1: Guild 3D 38
Ashbury Cres. GU4: Guild 2A 24
Ash Cl. GU2: Pyr 6E 6
GU22: Wok 4G 11
Ashcombe Pde. GU22: Wok 4J 11
(off Kingfield Rd.)
Ashcroft GU4: Shalf 4G 29
Ashdown Cl. GU22: Wok 2G 11
Ashenden Rd. GU2: Guild 4B 22
Ash Gro. GU2: Guild 4C 22
Ashley Ct. GU21: Wok 2B 10
Ashley Gdns. GU4: Shalf 4H 29
Ashley Ho. GU7: G'mng 6A 28
Ashley Rd. GU21: Wok 2B 10
Ashley Way GU2: W End 4D 2
Ash Rd. GU22: Wok 4F 11
GU24: Pirbr 3F 15
Ashstead La. GU7: G'mng 5J 33
Ashton Rd. GU21: Wok 1B 10
Ashtrees GU6: Cranl 7D 36
Ashwindham Ct. GU21: Wok 2B 10
Ashwood Pk. GU22: Wok 2J 11
Ashwood Pl. GU22: Wok 2J 11
Ashwood Rd. GU22: Wok 2H 11
Ashworth Pl. GU2: Guild 4B 22
Aspen Cl. GU4: Guild 1B 24
Astolat Bus. Pk., The
GU3: Peasm 5E 28
Astolat Way GU3: Peasm 5E 28
Astra Works GU6: Cranl 5B 36
Atherton Cl. GU4: Shalf 3G 29
Atkins Cl. GU21: Wok 2C 10
Atrium, The GU7: G'mng 3A 34
Attleford La. GU8: Shack 1A 32
August La. GU5: Alb 7H 31
Austen Rd. GU1: Guild 5H 23
Aven Cl. GU6: Cranl 6D 36
Avenue, The GU3: Comp 4J 27
GU3: Worp 4A 16
GU6: Ewh 7K 37
GU7: G'mng 5A 34
(The Drive)
GU7: G'mng 4J 27
(Withies La.)
GU18: Light 1A 2
GU24: Chob 1C 4
KT15: New H 1E 6
Avenue de Cagny GU24: Pirb 6F 9
Avenue Rd. GU6: Cranl 7D 36
Aviary Rd. GU22: Pyr 5F 6
Avington Cl. GU1: Guild 4G 23
Avonmead GU21: Wok 2E 10

Avonmore Av. GU1: Guild 3H 23
Avonmor M. GU23: Rip 6F 13
Avro Way KT13: Weyb 1J 7
Azalea Cl. GU22: Wok 3F 11

B

Bachelors La. GU23: Ock 1K 19
Back La. GU4: E Clan 1H 25
Back of High St. GU24: Chob 2A 4
Baden Powell Ct. GU7: G'mng 1K 33
Baden Rd. GU2: Guild 2C 22
Badger Cl. GU2: Guild 1D 22
Badger Dr. GU18: Light 1A 2
Badgers Cl. GU7: G'mng 6K 27
GU21: Wok 2E 10
Badgers Cross GU8: Mil 6F 33
Badgers Hollow GU7: G'mng 1K 33
Badger Wlk. GU3: Norm 5C 14
Bagmoor Common (Nature Reserve)
....6B 32
Bagshot Rd. GU3: Worp 5H 9
GU21: Knap 2H 9
GU22: Wok 5H 9
GU24: Brkwd, Wok 5H 9
GU24: Chob, W End 3E 2
Bailes La. GU3: Norm 1D 20
Baillie Rd. GU1: Guild 5H 23
Bainton Mead GU21: Wok 1C 10
Baird Dr. GU3: Woo V 3H 21
Bakersgate Courtyard
GU24: Pirb 2G 15
Bakersgate Gdns. GU24: Pirb 2G 15
Baker's Yd. GU1: Guild 4D 38 (5F 23)
Baldwin Cres. GU4: Guild 2A 24
Balfour Av. GU22: Wok 6G 11
Ballfield Rd. GU7: G'mng 1K 33
Balmoral Dr. GU22: Wok 7A 6
Bampton Way GU22: Wok 2C 10
Banders Ri. GU22: Wok 3A 24
Bankside GU21: Wok 2D 10
(not continuous)
Banks Way GU4: Burp 1H 23
Bannister's Rd. GU2: Guild 6B 22
Barataria Rd. GU23: Rip 5D 12
Barber Dr. GU6: Cranl 4D 36
Bardon Wlk. GU21: Wok 1D 10
Bargate Cl. GU2: Guild 4A 22
Bargate Ri. GU7: G'mng 3J 33
Barhatch La. GU6: Cranl 3E 36
Barhatch Rd. GU6: Cranl 3E 36
Barley Mow Cl. GU21: Knap 1K 9
Barley Mow La. GU21: Knap 7J 3
Barnard Ct. GU21: Wok 2A 10
Barnato Cl. KT14: Byfl 3J 7
Barnby Rd. GU21: Knap 1K 9
Barnes Rd. GU7: G'mng 6A 28
Barnes Wallis Dr. KT13: Weyb 2J 7
Barnett Cl. GU5: Wone 6A 30
Barnett La. GU5: Wone 6A 28
Barnett Row GU4: Jac W 6F 17
Barnfield GU6: Cranl 5D 36
Barnmead GU24: Chob 1B 4
Barns, The GU8: Shack 6C 26
Barnsbury Farm Est.
GU22: Wok 4F 11
Barnsford Cres. GU24: W End 4G 3
Barnwood Cl. GU2: Guild 2A 22
Barnwood Ct. GU2: Guild 2A 22
Barnwood Rd. GU2: Guild 3A 22
Barrack Path GU21: Wok 2A 10
(not continuous)
Barrack Rd. GU2: Guild 2C 22
Barrens Brae GU22: Wok 2J 11
Barrens Cl. GU22: Wok 3J 11
Barrens Pk. GU22: Wok 2J 11
Barricane GU21: Wok 3D 10
Barr's La. GU21: Knap 7K 3
(not continuous)
Bars, The GU1: Guild 3C 38 (5F 23)
Barton Cl. GU21: Knap 2J 9
Barton Pl. GU4: Burp 1K 23
Barton Rd. GU5: Bram 7J 29
Basset Cl. KT15: New H 1F 7
Bassett Rd. GU22: Wok 7A 6
Bateson Way GU21: Wok 5A 6
Batten Av. GU21: Wok 3A 10
Battersea Ct. GU22: Wok 4D 22
Bax Cl. GU6: Cranl 6D 36
Bayliss Ct. GU1: Guild 3B 38 (5E 22)
Baynton Rd. GU22: Wok 4K 11
Beacon Hill GU21: Wok 3E 10
Beaconsfield Rd. GU24: W End 4H 11
Beatty Av. GU1: Guild 3J 23
Beaufort Cl. GU22: Wok 7A 6
Beaufort M. GU22: Wok 2F 11
Beaufort Rd. GU22: Wok 7A 6
Beaumont Sq. GU6: Cranl 5E 36
Beavers Cl. GU3: Guild 3A 22

Beckingham Rd. GU2: Guild 2C 22
Bedford Cl. GU21: Wok 6E 4
Bedford Ho. GU1: Guild 3B 38 (5E 22)
Bedford Rd. GU1: Guild 3B 38 (5E 22)
Bedlow Cotts. GU6: Cranl 5E 36
Bedlow La. GU6: Cranl 5E 36
Bedser Cl. GU21: Wok 7J 5
Beech Cl. KT14: Byfl 3J 7
Beech Cl. GU1: Guild 5H 23
(off Easington Pl.)
Beechcroft Dr. GU2: Guild 7K 21
Beech Dr. GU23: Rip 1E 18
Beeches, The GU5: Bram 1H 35
Beech Gdns. GU22: Wok 6G 5
Beech Gro. GU2: Guild 4B 22
GU22: Wok 7F 11
GU24: Brkwd 4C 8
Beech Hill GU2: Guild 7A 38 (7E 22)
GU3: Flex 5A 20
Beech Lawn GU1: Guild 5H 23
Beechvale GU22: Wok 2H 11
(off Hill Vw. Rd.)
Beech Wlk. GU8: Mil 6F 33
Beech Way GU7: G'mng 4K 33
Beechway GU1: Guild 3K 23
Beechwood Cl. GU21: Knap 1A 10
Beechwood Rd. GU21: Knap 1A 10
Beggars La. GU24: Chob 2J 3
Beldam Bri. Rd.
GU24: Chob, W End 4G 3
Belgrave Mnr. GU22: Wok 3G 11
BELLFIELDS 7E 16
Bellfields Ct. GU1: Guild 7E 16
Bellfields Rd. GU1: Guild 6F 23
Belmont Av. GU2: Guild 1B 22
Belmont Pl. GU4: Burp 7K 17
Belmore Av. GU22: Pyr 7B 6
Belvedere Cl. GU2: Guild 2D 22
Benbrick Rd. GU2: Guild 5C 22
Benner La. GU24: W End 3F 3
Bennett Way GU4: W Cla 6E 18
Bentham Av. GU21: Wok 6A 6
Benwell Rd. GU24: Brkwd 3F 9
Berberis Cl. GU1: Guild 2E 22
(not continuous)
Bergenia Ct. GU24: W End 4E 2
Berkeley Gdns. KT14: W Byf 5D 6
Berkley Cl. GU2: Guild 4G 23
Berry La. GU3: Worp 2J 15
(not continuous)
Berrys Cl. KT14: Byfl 2H 7
Berry's La. KT14: Byfl 2H 7
Beta Rd. GU22: Wok 7K 5
GU24: Chob 1H 5
Bethany Pl. GU21: Wok 2F 11
Bicknell Cl. GU1: Guild 1C 38 (3E 22)
Bicton Cft. GU7: G'mng 1A 34
Big Apple, The
Woking 1H 11
Binfield Cl. KT14: Byfl 3K 7
Binfield Rd. KT14: Byfl 3J 7
Bingham Dr. GU21: Wok 2B 10
BINSCOMBE 6K 27
Binscombe GU7: G'mng 5K 27
Binscombe Cres. GU7: G'mng 7A 28
Binscombe La. GU7: G'mng 6K 27
Birchanger GU7: G'mng 3A 34
Birch Circ. GU7: G'mng 6B 28
Birch Cl. GU21: Wok 3E 10
GU23: Send 2D 18
Birchdale Cl. KT14: W Byf 2G 7
Birches, The GU22: Wok 2H 11
Birch Gro. GU1: Guild 1E 22
GU22: Pyr 6B 6
Birch La. GU24: W End 3D 2
Birchold Gro. GU7: G'mng 2B 34
Birch Platt GU24: W End 4D 2
Birch Tree Vw. GU18: Light 1A 2
Birch Wlk. KT14: W Byf 3E 6
(not continuous)
Birchwood Dr. GU18: Light 1C 2
KT14: W Byf 3E 6
Birchwood Rd. KT14: W Byf 3E 6
Birds Gro. GU21: Knap 2H 9
Birdswood Dr. GU21: Wok 3A 10
Birkin Ct. KT14: Byfl 2H 7
Birnam Ct. GU23: Rip 1E 18
Birtley Grn. GU5: Bram 2J 35
Birtley La. GU5: Bram 2J 35
Birtley Rd. GU5: Bram 2J 35
Bishops Cl. GU2: Guild 5B 38
Bishops Sq. GU6: Cranl 5E 36
Bishops Wharf GU1: Guild 4A 38
(off Walnut Tree Cl.)
Bishops Wood GU21: Wok 1B 10
BISLEY 6F 3

BISLEY CAMP 3D 8
Bisley Grn. GU24: Bisl 7F 3
Bitterne Dr. GU21: Wok 1B 10
Blackberry Cl. GU1: Guild 1D 22
Blackbridge Rd. GU22: Wok 3F 11
Blackburn Way GU7: G'mng 2B 34
Blackdown Av. GU22: Pyr 6C 6
Blackdown Cl. GU22: Pyr 7A 6
BLACKHEATH 5C 30
Blackheath 5D 30
Blackheath Gro. GU5: Wone 6K 29
Blackheath La. GU4: Blckh 6K 29
GU5: Alb 5F 31
GU5: Wone 6K 29
Blackmore Cres. GU21: Wok 6A 6
Blackness La. GU22: Wok 3G 11
Black Prince Cl. KT14: Byfl 5K 7
Blacksmith La. GU4: Shalf 6G 29
Blackstroud La. E. GU18: Light 2D 2
Blackstroud La. W. GU18: Light 2D 2
Blackthorn Dr. GU18: Light 3K 2
Blackthorn Pl. GU1: Guild 1E 22
Blackwell Av. GU2: Guild 4K 21
Blackwood Cl. KT14: W Byf 3G 7
Bladon Cl. GU1: Guild 3J 23
Blakes La. GU4: E Clan 2J 25
KT24: W Hor 1K 25
Blanchards Hill
GU4: Jac W, Sut G 5G 17
Blanchard Cl. GU22: Wok 1K 11
Blencarn Cl. GU21: Wok 7B 4
Blenheim Cl. KT14: W Byf 4D 6
Blenheim Gdns. GU22: Wok 3D 10
Blewfield GU7: Bus 5B 34
Blind La. GU24: Chob 1F 5
Bloggs Way GU6: Cranl 5C 36
Bloomfield Cl. GU21: Knap 1A 10
Bloomsbury Ct. GU1: Guild 6H 23
(off St Lukes Sq.)
Bloxham Rd. GU6: Cranl 5F 37
Bluebell Cott. GU3: Comp 5F 27
Bluebell Cl. GU22: Wok 3F 11
Bluebell Ri. GU18: Light 3B 2
Blunden Ct. GU5: Bram 1J 35
Board School Rd. GU21: Wok 7H 5
Bodeites GU7: G'mng 7H 27
Bolding Ho. La. GU24: W End 4F 3
Boleyn Ct. GU21: Knap 2J 9
(off Tudor Way)
Boltons Cl. GU22: Pyr 7E 6
Boltons La. GU22: Pyr 7E 6
Bonners Cl. GU22: Wok 6H 11
Bonsey Cl. GU22: Wok 5G 11
Bonsey La. GU22: Wok 5G 11
Bonseys La. GU24: Chob 1H 5
Bookham Hill GU6: Cranl 7K 27
Bookhurst Rd. GU6: Cranl, Ewh 4F 37
Borough Farm Rd. GU8: Mil 7A 32
Borough Hall Complex 3A 34
Borough Rd. GU7: G'mng 2K 33
Bothy, The GU8: P Har 2D 32
GU22: Pyr 1D 12
Boughton Hall Av. GU23: Send 1D 18
Boundary Bus. Cen. GU21: Wok 6J 5
Boundary Cotts. GU4: Guild 2E 30
Boundary Rd. GU21: Wok 6J 5
Boundary Way GU21: Wok 6J 5
Bourne Cl. GU4: Guild 3K 29
KT14: W Byf 4F 7
Bourne Rd. GU7: G'mng 6B 28
Bourne Way GU22: Wok 6F 11
Bower Ct. GU22: Wok 7K 5
Bowers Cl. GU4: Burp 7J 17
Bowers Farm Dr. GU4: Burp 7J 17
Bowers La. GU4: Burp 6J 17
Bowling Grn. GU3: Comp 4H 27
Bowling Grn. Rd. GU24: Chob 1A 4
Bowring Ho. GU7: G'mng 1B 34
(off St Johns St.)
Boxgrove Av. GU1: Guild 3J 23
Boxgrove La. GU1: Guild 3J 23
Boxgrove Rd. GU1: Guild 3J 23
Bracken Cl. GU5: Wone 1J 35
GU22: Wok 2H 11
Brackendene Cl. GU21: Wok 6J 5
Bracken La. GU6: Cranl 5G 37
Brackenlea GU7: G'mng 7K 27
Bracken Way GU3: Guild 2A 22
Brackenwood GU6: Cranl 5A 36
GU22: Wok 3K 9
Bradfield Cl. GU4: Burp 1J 23
Bradstone Brook GU4: Shalf 4J 29
Braemar Cl. GU7: G'mng 4K 33
Braeside KT15: New H 2F 7
Braganza Cl. GU1: Guild 6H 23
(off London Rd.)

Bramble Ct.—Chinthurst La.

Bramble Ct. GU6: Ewh 2K 37
Brambledene Cl. GU21: Wok 2E 10
Brambles, The GU7: G'mng 7K 27
Brambles Pk. GU5: Bram 1H 35
Bramble Way GU23: Rip 1D 18
BRAMLEY 1H 35
Bramley Bus. Cen. *GU5: Bram 7H 29*
(off Station Rd.)
Bramley Ct. GU24: Bisl 1H 9
Bramley Golf Course 7G 29
Bramley Grange GU5: Bram 1H 35
Bramley Pk. Ct. GU5: Bram 1H 35
Bramswell Rd. GU7: G'mng 1B 34
Brantwood Cl. KT14: W Byf 4E 6
Brantwood Ct. *KT14: W Byf 4D 6*
(off Brantwood Dr.)
Brantwood Dr. KT14: W Byf 4D 6
Brantwood Gdns. KT14: W Byf 4D 6
Bray Gdns. GU22: Pyr 7C 6
Bray Rd. GU2: Guild 5D 22
Brentmoor Rd. GU24: W End 4C 2
Brewery La. KT14: Byfl 4J 7
Brewery Rd. GU21: Wok 1F 11
Briar Av. GU18: Light 3A 2
Briar Cl. KT14: W Byf 2F 7
Briar Ct. GU24: Bisl 1H 9
Briar Patch GU7: G'mng 1K 33
Briar Rd. GU23: Send 1K 17
Briar Wlk. KT14: W Byf 3E 6
Briar Way GU4: Burp 7K 17
Briarwood Rd. GU21: Wok 3K 9
Brickfield Cotts. GU3: Flex 4D 20
Bricks La. GU3: Art 4D 28
Bridge Barn La. GU21: Wok 2F 11
Bridge Cl. GU21: Wok 1E 10
KT14: Byfl 3K 7
Bridge Ct. GU21: Wok 1F 11
Bridgehill Cl. GU2: Guild 2C 22
Bridge Mead GU24: Pirb 3F 15
Bridge M. GU7: G'mng 3A 34
GU21: Wok 1F 11
Bridge Pk. GU4: Guild 1A 24
Bridge Rd. GU6: Cranl 6D 36
GU7: G'mng 2A 34
Bridge St. GU1: Guild 4B 38 (5E 22)
GU7: G'mng 3A 34
Bridge St. Pas. GU1: Guild 4B 38
Bridgewater GU21: Wok 7H 5
Brierly Cl. GU2: Guild 2C 22
Bright Hill GU1: Guild 5D 38 (6G 23)
Brighton Rd. GU7: Bus, G'mng 3A 34
Brind Cotts. GU24: Chob 1B 4
Brittens Cl. GU2: Guild 6C 16
Broad Acres GU7: G'mng 6A 28
Broadacres GU3: Guild 2A 22
BROADFORD 4F 29
Broadford La. GU24: Chob 3A 4
Broadford Pk. GU4: Shalf 4F 29
Broadford Pk. Bus. Cen.
GU4: Shalf 4F 29
Broadford Rd. GU3: Peasm 5E 28
GU4: Shalf 5E 28
Broadmead Rd. GU22: Wok 6K 11
GU23: Send 6K 11
Broadmeads GU23: Send 6K 11
Broadoaks Cres. KT14: W Byf 4F 7
Broad St. GU3: Guild, Woo V 2J 21
GU24: W End 4D 2
BROAD STREET COMMON 1K 21
Broad Wlk. GU6: Cranl 7E 36
Broadwater Cl. GU21: Wok 3B 6
Broadwater La. GU7: G'mng 1B 34
Broadwater Pk. Golf Course 7C 28
Broadwater Ri. GU1: Guild 5J 23
Broadway GU21: Knap 2H 9
Broadway, The GU21: Wok 1H 11
KT15: New H 1E 6
Broadway Ct. GU21: Knap 1J 9
Broadway Ho. GU21: Knap 2J 9
Broadway Rd. GU18: Light 1C 2
Brockenhurst Cl. GU21: Wok 5H 5
Brockhill GU21: Wok 1C 10
Brocks Cl. GU7: G'mng 2C 34
Brocks Dr. GU3: Worp 7J 15
Brockway Cl. GU1: Guild 3K 23
Brodie Rd. GU1: Guild 4E 38 (5G 23)
Broke Ct. GU4: Guild 1A 24
Bronlei Woods GU5: Bram 3K 35
BROOK 5J 31
Brooke Forest GU3: Worp 7J 15
Brookfield GU7: G'mng 6C 28
GU21: Wok 7D 4
Brook Grn. *GU24: Chob 1B 4*
(off Chertsey Rd.)
Brook Hill GU5: Alb 6H 31
Brook Ho. GU6: Cranl 4E 36
BROOKLANDS 1K 7
Brooklands Bus. Pk. KT13: Weyb 2J 7
Brooklands Ct. KT15: New H 1H 7
Brooklands Dr. KT13: Weyb 1K 7
Brooklands Ind. Est. KT13: Weyb 1J 7
Brooklands Rd. KT13: Weyb 3K 7
Brook La. GU5: Alb 5J 31
GU23: Send 6C 12
GU24: Chob 2K 3
Brookleys GU24: Chob 1B 4
Brooklyn Cl. GU22: Wok 3G 11
Brooklyn Ct. GU22: Wok 3G 11
Brooklyn Rd. GU22: Wok 2G 11
Brook Mead GU8: Mil 7F 33
Brookmead Ct. GU6: Cranl 6D 36
Brook Rd. GU4: Guild 4A 30
Brookside GU4: Jac W 6F 17
GU6: Cranl 5D 36
(Ewhurst Rd.)
GU6: Cranl 7D 36
(Waverleigh Rd.)
Brookwell La. GU5: Bram 6J 35
BROOKWOOD 4G 9
Brookwood Country Pk. 3J 9
Brookwood Farm GU21: Brkwd 3G 9
Brookwood Farm Dr.
GU21: Knap 3H 9
Brookwood Lye Rd.
GU24: Brkwd 4H 9
Brookwood Station (Rail) 5G 9
Broomcroft Cl. GU22: Pyr 7B 6
Broomcroft Dr. GU22: Pyr 6B 6
Broomers La. GU6: Ewh 3K 37
Broom Fld. GU18: Light 3A 2
Broomfield GU2: Guild 3A 22
Broomfield Cl. GU3: Guild 2A 22
Broomfield Rd. KT15: New H 2F 7
Broomhall End *GU21: Wok 7G 5*
(off Broomhall La.)
Broomhall La. GU21: Wok 7G 5
Broomhall Rd. GU21: Wok 7G 5
Browell Ho. *GU4: Guild 3B 24*
(off Merrow St.)
Browne Cl. GU22: Wok 4K 11
Brox La. KT16: Ott 1B 6
Bruce Cl. KT14: Byfl 4H 7
Brunswick Dr. GU24: Brkwd 4D 8
Brunswick Rd. GU24: Brkwd 5A 8
(not continuous)
Brushfield Way GU21: Knap 3J 9
Bryanstone Av. GU2: Guild 7B 16
Bryanstone Cl. GU2: Guild 1B 22
Bryanstone Gro. GU2: Guild 7B 16
Bryant M. GU4: Shalf 3G 29
Brynford Cl. GU21: Wok 6G 5
Bryony Rd. GU1: Guild 1K 23
Buckingham Cl. GU1: Guild 3H 23
Bucks Cl. KT14: W Byf 5F 7
Bullard Cotts. GU4: W Cla 2D 24
Bullbeggars La. GU21: Wok 7D 4
BULLSWATER COMMON 3G 15
Bullswater Comn. Rd.
GU24: Pirb 3G 15
Bullswater La. GU24: Pirb 2G 15
Bungalows, The GU2: Guild 6B 16
Bunyan's La. GU24: Chob 5J 3
Bunyard Dr. GU21: Wok 5A 6
Burdenshot Hill GU3: Worp 2C 16
Burdenshott Rd. GU3: Worp 2C 16
Burden Way GU2: Guild 6D 16
Burdock Cl. GU18: Light 2B 2
Burleigh Gdns. GU21: Wok 1H 11
Burlingham Cl. GU4: Guild 2B 24
Burnet Av. GU1: Guild 1K 23
Burnet Cl. GU24: W End 4E 2
Burnham Cl. GU21: Knap 2K 9
Burnham Ga.
GU1: Guild 1C 38 (4F 23)
Burnham Rd. GU21: Knap 2K 9
BURNTCOMMON 2D 18
Burnt Comn. Cl. GU23: Rip 2D 18
Burnt Comn. La. GU23: Rip 2E 18
Burnt Pollard La. GU18: Light 1E 2
BURPHAM 1K 23
Burpham La. GU4: Burp 6J 17
Burr Hill La. GU24: Chob 1B 4
BURROW HILL 6E 8
BURROWHILL 1A 4
Burrows Cl. GU2: Guild 3B 22
Burton Dr. GU3: Worp 6G 15
Burwood Cl. GU1: Guild 3B 24
Bury Cl. GU21: Wok 7F 5
Bury Flds. GU2: Guild 6B 38 (6E 22)
Bury La. GU21: Wok 7E 4
Bury M. GU2: Guild 6B 38
Burys, The GU7: G'mng 2A 34
Bury St. GU2: Guild 6B 38 (6E 22)
BUSBRIDGE 5B 34
Busbridge Lakes, Waterfowl & Gdns.
6A 34
Busbridge La. GU7: G'mng 4K 33
Busdens Cl. GU8: Mil 7F 33
Busdens La. GU8: Mil 7F 33
Busdens Way GU8: Mil 7F 33
Bush La. GU23: Send 1B 18
BUSHY HILL 3B 24
Bushy Hill Dr. GU1: Guild 2K 23
Butler's Pl. GU8: Mil 6G 33
Butt Cl. GU6: Cranl 4D 36
Butt La. GU3: Putt 1A 26
Butts La. GU7: G'mng 3K 33
Butts Rd. GU21: Wok 1G 11
BYFLEET 3J 7
Byfleet & New Haw Station
(Rail) 1H 7
Byfleet Ind. Est. KT14: Byfl 1H 7
Byfleet Rd. KT14: Byfl 3K 7
KT15: New H 1H 7
Byfleet Technical Cen.
KT14: Byfl 2H 7
Bylands GU22: Wok 3J 11
Byrefield Rd. GU2: Guild 1B 22
Byron Cl. GU21: Knap 1A 10

C

Cabell Rd. GU2: Guild 3K 21
Cable Ho. Ct. GU21: Wok 6G 5
Cadogan Ho. *GU1: Guild 5H 23*
(off St Lukes Sq.)
Caillard Rd. KT14: Byfl 2J 7
Caledon Pl. GU4: Burp 1J 23
Calluna Ct. GU22: Wok 2H 11
Camargue Pl. GU7: G'mng 3B 34
Cambridge Cl. GU21: Wok 2B 10
Camellia Ct. GU24: W End 4F 3
Cameron Cl. GU6: Cranl 7D 36
Campbell Av. GU22: Wok 5H 11
Campbell Cir. KT13: Weyb 1K 7
Campbell Cl. KT14: Byfl 3H 7
Camphill Ct. KT14: W Byf 3E 6
Camphill Ind. Est. KT14: W Byf 2F 7
Camphill Rd. KT14: W Byf 3E 6
Canada Copse GU8: Mil 5E 32
Canada Rd. KT14: Byfl 2H 7
Canal Bank M. GU21: Wok 1G 11
Candlerush Cl. GU22: Wok 1K 11
Canewdon Cl. GU22: Wok 3G 11
Canfold Cotts. GU6: Cranl 4G 37
Cannon Cres. GU24: Chob 2A 4
Canterbury Rd. GU2: Guild 2B 22
Canvil Pl. GU6: Cranl 4F 37
Capital Pk. GU22: Wok 5K 11
Capstans Wharf GU21: Wok 2B 10
Caradon Cl. GU21: Wok 2D 10
Caraway Pl. GU2: Guild 6C 16
Cardamom Cl. GU2: Guild 7C 16
Cardigan Cl. GU21: Wok 2A 10
Cardinal Pl. GU22: Wok 2G 11
Cardingham GU21: Wok 1C 10
Cardwells Keep GU2: Guild 1C 22
Carlos St. GU7: G'mng 3A 34
Carlton Cl. GU21: Wok 5H 5
Carlton Rd. GU21: Wok 5J 5
Carmel Cl. GU22: Wok 2G 11
Carolyn Cl. GU21: Wok 3B 10
Carroll Av. GU1: Guild 4K 23
CARTBRIDGE 6K 11
Cartbridge Cl. GU23: Send 7K 11
Carters Cl. GU1: Guild 7G 17
Carters La. GU22: Wok 4A 12
Carthouse Cotts. GU4: Guild 1A 24
Carthouse La. GU21: Wok 5K 3
CASTLE GREEN 4K 3
Castle Gro. Rd. GU24: Chob 4K 3
Castle Hill GU1: Guild 6C 38 (6F 23)
Castle Rd. GU21: Wok 5H 5
Castle Sq. GU1: Guild 5D 38 (6F 23)
Castle St. GU1: Guild 5C 38 (6F 23)
Catalpa Cl. GU1: Guild 2E 22
Catena Ri. GU18: Light 1A 2
Cater Gdns. GU3: Guild 2B 22
Caterham Cl. GU24: Pirb 5E 8
Cathedral Cl. GU2: Guild 5D 22
Cathedral Ct. GU2: Guild 4C 22
Cathedral Hill GU2: Guild 3C 22
Cathedral Hill Ind. Est.
GU2: Guild 3C 22
Cathedral Pl. *GU1: Guild 1C 38*
(off Markenfield Rd.)
Cathedral Vw. GU2: Guild 4B 22
Catherine Cl. KT14: Byfl 5J 7
CATTESHALL 2C 34
Catteshall Hatch GU7: G'mng 1C 34
Catteshall La. GU7: G'mng 3A 34
Catteshall Rd. GU7: G'mng 1C 34
(not continuous)
Catteshall Ter. *GU7: G'mng 2C 34*
(off Catteshall Rd.)
Causeway Ct. GU21: Wok 2B 10
Cavell Way GU21: Knap 3J 9
Cavendish Rd. GU22: Wok 3F 11
Cavenham Cl. GU22: Wok 3G 11
Cawsey Way GU21: Wok 1G 11
Caxton Gdns. GU2: Guild 3D 22
Cedar Gdns. GU21: Wok 2D 10
GU24: Chob 1B 4
Cedar Gro. GU24: Bisl 6G 3
Cedar Ho. GU4: Guild 2A 24
Cedar Rd. GU22: Wok 4D 10
Cedars, The GU1: Burp 1J 23
GU8: Mil 7E 32
GU24: Pirb 6D 8
KT14: Byfl 3K 7
Cedars Ct. GU1: Burp 1J 23
Cedar Way GU1: Guild 2E 22
Celtic Rd. KT14: Byfl 5J 7
Cemetery Pales GU24: Brkwd 6F 9
Centrium GU22: Wok 1H 11
Century Ct. GU21: Wok 7H 5
Century Way GU24: Brkwd 3D 8
Chalk La. GU8: Shack 6D 26
Chalk Rd. GU7: G'mng 2K 33
Chancellor Ct. GU2: Guild 5K 21
(not continuous)
Chandlers Cl. *GU21: Wok 2B 10*
(off Robin Hood Rd.)
Channings GU21: Wok 6G 5
Chantry Cotts. GU4: Guild 3K 29
Chantry La. GU5: Shere 2K 31
Chantry Quarry
GU1: Guild 7D 38 (7F 23)
Chantry Rd. GU4: Guild 3K 29
Chantry Vw. Rd.
GU1: Guild 7D 38 (7F 23)
Chapel Cl. GU8: Mil 5F 33
Chapel Ct. GU8: Mil 6F 33
Chapel Farm Mobile Home Pk.
GU3: Norm 1E 20
Chapel Flds. GU7: G'mng 7K 27
Chapelhouse Cl. GU2: Guild 4A 22
Chapel La. GU8: Mil 5F 33
GU24: Pirb 6G 9
Chapel St. GU1: Guild 5C 38 (6F 23)
GU21: Wok 1H 11
Charlock Way GU1: Guild 1K 23
Charlotte Ct. GU1: Guild 6H 23
Charlotte Ter. *GU1: Guild 6G 23*
(off Addison Rd.)
CHARLOTTEVILLE 6H 23
CHARTERHOUSE 7J 27
Charterhouse GU7: G'mng 1H 33
Charterhouse Club 7H 27
Charterhouse Rd. GU7: G'mng 7K 27
Charterhouse School Golf Course
7G 27
Charts Cl. GU6: Cranl 6D 36
Chartwell *GU22: Wok 2G 11*
(off Mt. Hermon Rd.)
Chase, The GU2: Guild 5C 22
Chasefield Cl. GU4: Burp 1J 23
Chatfield Dr. GU4: Guild 2A 24
Chatham M. GU2: Guild 1C 22
Chatton Row GU24: Bisl 1G 9
Chaucer Ct. GU2: Guild 6B 38 (6E 22)
Chaucer Ho. GU1: Guild 5H 23
Cheapside GU21: Wok 5F 5
Cheniston Cl. KT14: W Byf 4E 6
Chequer Tree Cl. GU21: Knap 7A 4
Cherry St. GU21: Wok 2G 11
Cherry Tree Av. GU2: Guild 4B 22
Cherry Tree La. GU7: G'mng 6K 27
Cherry Tree Rd. GU8: Mil 6E 32
Chertsey Rd. GU21: Wok 1H 11
GU24: Chob 1B 4
KT14: Byfl 2H 7
Chertsey St. GU1: Guild 4D 38 (5F 23)
Cheselden Rd.
GU1: Guild 4E 38 (5G 23)
Chesham M. GU1: Guild 5G 23
Chesham Rd. GU1: Guild 5H 23
Chester Cl. GU2: Guild 2B 22
Chestnut Av. GU2: Guild 7E 22
Chestnut Cl. GU23: Rip 2D 18
Chestnut Gro. GU22: Wok 4G 11
Chestnut Rd.
GU1: Guild 1C 38 (4F 23)
Chestnut Wlk. KT14: Byfl 3J 7
Chestnut Way GU5: Bram 2J 35
GU7: Bus 5B 34
Chevremont GU1: Guild 5G 23
Cheyne Row GU5: Bram 7F 35
Chiltern Cl. GU22: Wok 6E 10
CHILWORTH 3A 30
Chilworth Hill Cotts.
GU4: Guild 4C 30
Chilworth Manor 2B 30
Chilworth Rd. GU5: Alb 2E 30
Chilworth Station (Rail) 3C 30
Chinthurst Hill Nature Reserve 6J 29
Chinthurst Hill Tower 6J 29
Chinthurst La. GU4: Shalf 4G 29
GU5: Bram, Wone 4G 29

A-Z Guildford & Woking 41

Chinthurst Pk. GU4: Shalf 5G 29
Chipstead Ct. GU21: Knap 1A 10
Chirton Wlk. GU21: Wok 2C 10
Chittenden Cotts. GU23: Wis 7J 7
CHITTYS COMMON 7B 16
Chittys Wlk. GU3: Guild 7B 16
CHOBHAM 2A 4
Chobham Bus. Cen.
  GU24: Chob 1F 5
Chobham Golf Course 6K 3
Chobham Mus. 2A 4
Chobham Pk. La. GU24: Chob 1C 4
Chobham Rd. GU21: Knap, Wok 2H 9
  GU21: Wok 4E 4
    (Horsell Comn. Rd.)
  GU21: Wok 7G 5
    (Wheatsheaf Cl., not continuous)
Choir Grn. GU21: Knap 1A 10
Christchurch Way
  .....1H 11
Christie Cl. GU1: Guild 1F 23
  GU18: Light 1C 2
Christmas Hill GU4: Shalf 4H 29
    (not continuous)
  GU5: Wone 4H 29
Christmas Pie Av. GU3: Flex 4B 20
CHRISTOPHER'S
  CHILDREN'S HOSPICE
  (SHOOTING STAR CHASE)
  .....2E 28
Christ's College Ski Club 1D 22
Church Cl. GU4: Shalf 2F 29
  GU8: Mil 6F 33
  GU21: Wok 7F 5
  GU21: Brkwd 5F 9
CHURCH END 5K 13
Churchfields GU4: Burp 6J 17
  GU21: Wok 7G 5
Church Hill GU21: Wok 7F 5
  GU22: Pyr 1D 12
Churchill Rd. GU1: Guild 5G 23
Church La. GU3: Worp 4A 16
  GU5: Alb 2F 31
  GU6: Cranl 5D 36
  GU23: Send 3K 17
  GU24: Bisl 6G 3
  GU24: Pirb 0D 8
Church Path GU21: Wok 1H 11
Church Rd.
  GU1: Guild 3C 38 (5F 23)
  GU8: Mil 7F 33
  GU21: Wok 6G 5
    (Beech Lawn)
  GU21: Wok 3C 10
    (St John's Hill Rd.)
Dene Cl. GU4: W End 3F 3
  KT14: Byfl 5J 7
Church St. GU4: Guild 6F 17
Church St. E. GU21: Wok 1H 11
Church St. W. GU21: Wok 1G 11
Church Wlk. GU7: G'mng 1B 34
Chuters Cl. KT14: Byfl 3J 7
Cinder Path GU22: Wok 3E 10
Cinnamon Gdns. GU2: Guild 6C 16
Circle, The GU7: G'mng 1B 34
Circle Gdns. KT13: Weyb 4K 7
Circuit Cen., The KT13: Weyb 2J 7
Clandon Ho. GU1: Guild 6J 23
CLANDON PARK 2E 24
Clandon Pk. 7D 18
Clandon Regis Golf Course 1F 25
Clandon Rd. GU1: Guild 5G 23
  GU4: W Cla 2D 18
  GU23: Send 2D 18
Clandon Station (Rail) 6F 19
Clappers La. GU24: Chob 2J 3
Clare Cl. KT14: W Byf 4E 6
Claredale GU22: Wok 3G 11
Claremont Av. GU22: Wok 3G 11
Claremont Dr. GU22: Wok 3G 11
Claremont Rd. KT14: W Byf 3E 6
Claydon Rd. GU21: Wok 7C 4
Clayhanger GU4: Guild 2A 24
Clay La. GU4: Burp, Jac W 5F 17
Clayton Dr. GU2: Guild 1B 22
Cleardown GU22: Wok 2K 11
Clearsprings GU18: Light 1A 2
Cleeve, The GU1: Guild 4J 23
Clew's La. GU24: Bisl 7G 3
Cliffe Ri. GU1: G'mng 4J 33
Cliffe Rd. GU7: G'mng 5H 33
Clifford Mnr. Rd. GU4: Guild 1G 29
Clifton Way GU21: Wok 1B 10
Cline Rd. GU1: Guild 4H 23
Clinton Cl. GU21: Knap 2K 9
Clock Ho. Cl. KT14: Byfl 3K 7
Clockhouse Ct. GU1: Guild 7E 16
Clock Ho. La. GU5: Bram 1H 35
Clodhouse Hill GU22: Wok 6K 9

Cloisters, The GU1: Burp 7J 17
  GU22: Wok 5K 11
Close, The GU5: Wone 7K 29
  GU7: G'mng 4B 34
  GU18: Light 1A 2
  KT14: W Byf 4E 6
Clover Ct. GU22: Wok 2F 11
Clover Lea GU7: G'mng 6A 28
Clover Rd. GU3: Guild 3A 22
Club Row GU24: Brkwd 3D 8
Coachlads Av. GU2: Guild 4B 22
Coatham Pl. GU6: Cranl 5E 36
Cobbett Hill Rd. GU3: Norm 5E 14
Cobbett Rd. GU2: Guild 3B 22
Cobbetts Cl. GU3: Norm 6F 15
  GU21: Wok 1D 10
Cobbetts Farm GU24: Bisl 6G 3
Cobbetts Wlk. GU24: Bisl 6G 3
Cobblett Pk. GU1: Guild 7G 17
Cobs Way KT15: New H 1G 7
Codrington Ct. GU21: Wok 2B 10
Colburn Cres. GU4: Burp 1J 23
Coldharbour La. GU22: Pyr 6D 6
  GU24: W End 2F 3
Coldharbour Rd. GU22: Pyr 6D 6
  KT14: W Byf 5D 6
Coley Av. GU22: Wok 2J 11
College Hill GU7: G'mng 4J 33
College La. GU22: Wok 3E 10
College Rd. GU1: Guild 3C 38 (5F 23)
  GU22: Wok 7K 5
Collens Fld. GU24: Pirb 1F 15
Colliers Cl. GU21: Wok 1D 10
Collier Way GU4: Guild 2B 24
Collingdon GU6: Cranl 7E 36
Collingwood Cres. GU1: Guild 3J 23
Coltsfoot Dr. GU1: Guild 1J 23
Colville Gdns. GU18: Light 2C 2
Colyton Cl. GU21: Wok 2E 10
Combe La. GU5: Shere 7K 25
  GU8: Bus 5E 34
Combe Rd. GU7: G'mng 6A 28
Comeragh Cl. GU22: Wok 4C 10
Commercial Rd.
  GU1: Guild 4C 38 (5F 23)
Commercial Way GU21: Wok 1G 11
COMMON, THE 4J 27
Common, The GU4: Shalf 4G 29
  GU5: Wone 6K 29
  GU6: Cranl 5B 36
    (not continuous)
Common Cl. GU21: Wok 5F 5
Commonfields GU24: W End 3G 3
Common La. GU4: W End 6D 2
  KT15: New H 1G 7
COMPTON 3H 27
Compton Cl. GU1: Guild 5H 23
Compton Hgts. GU3: Guild 7K 21
Condor Ct. GU2: Guild 6B 38 (6E 22)
Coneyhurst La. GU6: Ewh 1H 37
Conford Dr. GU4: Shalf 4G 29
Coniers Way GU4: Burp 1K 23
Conista Ct. GU21: Wok 7B 4
Coniston Ct. GU18: Light 1B 2
Coniston Rd. GU22: Wok 4K 11
Connaught Cres. GU24: Brkwd 4F 9
Connaught Dr. KT13: Weyb 2K 7
Connaught Rd. GU24: Brkwd 5E 8
Consort Ct. GU22: Wok 2G 11
Constitution Hill GU22: Wok 3G 11
Convent Cl. GU21: Wok 1K 11
Cook Way GU2: Guild 3K 21
COOMBE BOTTOM 7K 25
Coombe La. GU3: Worp 6J 15
    (not continuous)
Coombe Mnr. GU24: Bisl 6G 3
Coombes, The GU5: Bram 2J 35
Coombe Way KT14: Byfl 3K 7
Cooper Rd. GU1: Guild 6H 23
Coopers Hill Dr. GU24: Brkwd 4C 8
Coopers Ri. GU7: G'mng 4H 33
Copley Cl. GU21: Wok 3A 10
Copper Beech Cl. GU22: Wok 5D 10
Copper Beech Ho. GU22: Wok 1H 11
Coppice Cl. GU2: Guild 3K 21
Coppice End GU22: Pyr 7C 6
Copse, The GU6: Cranl 5F 37
  GU23: Send 1D 18
Copse Cl. GU1: Guild 3A 30
Copse Edge GU6: Cranl 4E 36
Copse Rd. GU21: Wok 2B 10
Copse Side GU7: G'mng 6K 27
Copthall Way KT15: New H 1D 6
Copthorne Dr. GU18: Light 1B 2
Coresbrook Way GU21: Knap 2G 9
Coriander Cres. GU2: Guild 6C 16
Corner, The KT14: W Byf 4E 6
Corner Bungs. GU7: Hurt 6H 27
Cornfields GU7: G'mng 6B 28
Cornwall Av. KT14: Byfl 5K 7

Corrie Rd. GU22: Wok 4K 11
Cottage Wlk. GU7: G'mng 3A 34
Cottesloe Cl. GU24: Bisl 7F 3
Cotts Wood Dr. GU4: Burp 6J 17
Council Cotts. GU23: Wis 6H 7
  GU24: W End 3F 3
County Court
  Guildford 3B 38 (5E 22)
Court, The GU2: Guild 6B 38 (6E 22)
Courtenay M. GU21: Wok 7J 5
Courtenay Rd. GU21: Wok 7J 5
Court Grn. Hgts. GU22: Wok 4E 10
Courtyard, The KT14: W Byf 3K 6
Courtyard M. GU5: Bram 1J 35
Cowbridge Mdw. GU24: Pirb 7F 9
Cow La. GU7: G'mng 3K 33
COWSHOT COMMON 4E 8
Cowshot Cres. GU24: Brkwd 4D 8
Cowslip La. GU21: Wok 6D 4
Coyne Cl. GU18: Light 1C 2
Craggy Island 7F 17
Craigmore Twr. GU22: Wok 3G 11
    (off Constitution Hill)
Cranbrook Ter. GU6: Cranl 6E 36
Cranfield Cl. GU21: Wok 2C 10
CRANLEIGH 5C 36
Cranleigh Arts Cen. 5D 36
Cranleigh Golf Course 2E 36
Cranleigh Leisure Cen. 6C 36
Cranleigh Mead GU6: Cranl 6E 36
Cranleigh Rd. GU5: Wone 7K 29
  GU6: Ewh 4J 37
Cranley Cl. GU1: Guild 4J 23
Cranley Dene GU1: Guild 4J 23
Cranley Pl. GU21: Knap 2K 9
Cranley Rd. GU1: Guild 4H 23
Cranmer Ct. GU21: Knap 2J 9
    (off Hampton Cl.)
Cranstoun Cl. GU3: Guild 7B 16
Crescent, The GU2: Guild 3C 22
Cresta Dr. KT15: Wdhm 1D 6
Creston Av. GU21: Knap 7A 4
Creswell GU21: Wok 1K 9
Creswell Cnr. GU21: Knap 1K 9
Cricketers Cl. GU22: Wok 5G 11
Cricket Grn. Cl. GU8: Shack 7C 26
CRICKETS HILL 2K 17
Cricketts Hill GU5: Shere 2K 31
Crockery La. GU4: E Clan 6H 19
Croft Rd. GU22: Wok 3K 33
Cromar Ct. GU21: Wok 7E 4
Cromwell Ct. GU21: Knap 3J 9
    (off Tudor Way)
Cromwell Pl. GU6: Cranl 7E 36
Crossacres GU22: Pyr 7C 6
Cross Lanes GU1: Guild 4H 23
Crossways, The GU2: Guild 6B 22
Crowcroft Cl. GU2: Guild 7D 16
Crown Court
  Guildford 3B 38 (5E 22)
Crown Ct. GU7: G'mng 3A 34
Crown Hgts.
  GU1: Guild 7E 38 (7G 23)
CROWNPITS 4B 34
Crownpits La. GU7: G'mng 4A 34
Crown Sq. GU21: Wok 1H 11
    (off Chertsey Rd.)
Crown Wlk. GU7: G'mng 3A 34
Cubitt Cl. GU7: G'mng 1B 34
Cubitt Ho. GU6: Cranl 4B 36
Cubitt Way GU21: Knap 2K 9
Cuckoo La. GU24: W End 4D 2
Cuckoo Va. GU24: W End 4D 2
Cull's Rd. GU3: Flex 4B 20
Culver Ho. GU1: Guild 4J 23
Culworth Ho. GU1: Guild 5G 23
Cumberland Av. GU2: Guild 6C 16
Cunningham Av. GU1: Guild 3J 23
Cunningham Cl. GU3: Flex 4B 20
Curlew Gdns. GU4: Guild 2B 24
Curling Va. GU2: Guild 6C 22
Cygnet Cl. GU21: Wok 7D 4
Cypress Rd. GU1: Guild 2E 22

D

Daffodil Dr. GU24: Bisl 7G 3
Dagden Rd. GU4: Shalf 3G 29
Dagley Farm Pk. Homes
  GU4: Shalf 3F 29
Dagley La. GU4: Shalf 2F 29
Dairyman's Wlk. GU4: Burp 6K 17
Dale Vw. GU21: Wok 2D 10
Damask Cl. GU24: W End 4E 2
Dane Ct. GU22: Pyr 6D 6
Danesfield GU23: Rip, Send 7D 12
Danes Hill GU22: Wok 2J 11
Danesrood GU1: Guild 5H 23
Danone Ct. GU1: Guild 2C 38

Danses Cl. GU4: Guild 2B 24
Dapdune Ct.
  GU1: Guild 2B 38 (4E 22)
Dapdune Rd.
  GU1: Guild 2C 38 (4F 23)
Dapdune Wharf 2A 38 (4E 22)
Dapdune Wharf Vis. Cen.
  .....2B 38 (4E 22)
Daphne Jackson Rd.
  GU2: Guild 5A 22
Darfield Rd. GU4: Guild 1J 23
Dark La. GU3: Putt 2B 26
  GU5: Shere 2K 31
Dartmouth Av. GU21: Wok 5A 6
Dartmouth Grn. GU21: Wok 5B 6
Dartmouth Path GU21: Wok 5B 6
Dartnell Av. KT14: W Byf 3F 7
Dartnell Cl. KT14: W Byf 3F 7
Dartnell Ct. KT14: W Byf 3G 7
Dartnell Cres. KT14: W Byf 3F 7
DARTNELL PARK 3F 7
Dartnell Pk. Rd. KT14: W Byf 3F 7
Dartnell Pl. KT14: W Byf 3F 7
Darvel Cl. GU21: Wok 7C 4
Daryngton Dr. GU1: Guild 4K 23
Dashwood Cl. KT14: W Byf 3G 7
David Lloyd Leisure
  Woking 4H 11
Davies Cl. GU7: G'mng 7K 27
Daviesites GU7: G'mng 7H 27
Davis Rd. KT13: Weyb 1K 7
Davos Cl. GU22: Wok 3G 11
Dawney Hill GU24: Pirb 5E 8
Dawneys Rd. GU24: Pirb 6E 8
Dawson Rd. KT14: Byfl 2H 7
Dayspring GU2: Guild 7D 16
Deacon Fld. GU2: Guild 3C 22
Deanery Pl. GU7: G'mng 3K 33
    (off Church St.)
Deanery Rd. GU7: G'mng 2K 33
Dean Rd. GU7: G'mng 1K 33
Dedswell Dr. GU4: W Cla 6E 18
Deep Pool La. GU24: Wok 5D 4
Deeprose Cl. GU2: Guild 7D 16
Deerbarn Rd. GU2: Guild 3D 22
Deer Leap GU18: Light 2A 2
Deers Farm Cl. GU23: Wis 7J 7
De Havilland Dr. KT13: Weyb 2J 7
De Lara Way GU21: Wok 2F 11
Dell, The GU21: Wok 3E 10
Delta Cl. GU24: Chob 1B 4
Delta Rd. GU21: Wok 7J 5
  GU24: Chob 1B 4
Denby Rd. GU1: Guild 1K 23
Denehyrst Ct. GU1: Guild 5G 23
    (off York Rd.)
Denelea Ct. GU6: Cranl 5A 36
Dene Pl. GU21: Wok 2E 10
Dene Rd. GU1: Guild 3E 38 (5G 23)
Denholm Gdns. GU4: Burp 1J 23
Denly Way GU18: Light 1C 2
Denmark Rd.
  GU1: Guild 3E 38 (5G 23)
DENNISVILLE 5C 22
Dennis Way GU1: Guild 6G 17
Denton Way GU21: Wok 1B 10
Denvale Wlk. GU21: Wok 2C 10
Denzil Rd. GU2: Guild 4A 38 (5D 22)
Derby Rd. GU2: Guild 4B 22
Derisley Cl. KT14: Byfl 3H 7
Derrydown Rd. GU21: Wok 5E 10
Derwent Rd. GU18: Light 2B 2
Devoil Cl. GU4: Burp 7K 17
Devon Bank GU2: Guild 7B 38 (7E 22)
Devonshire Av. GU21: Wok 5A 6
Dewlands Cl. GU6: Cranl 5D 36
Dewlands La. GU6: Cranl 5D 36
Dianthus Ct. GU22: Wok 2F 11
Digby Way KT14: Byfl 3K 7
Dillon Cotts. GU4: Burp 6A 18
Dinsdale Cl. GU22: Wok 2J 11
Dixon Dr. KT13: Weyb 1K 7
Dodds Cres. KT14: W Byf 5F 7
Dodd's La. GU22: Pyr 5E 6
DONKEY TOWN 4D 2
Donnafields GU24: Bisl 7G 3
Donne Gdns. GU22: Pyr 6C 6
Dorchester Ct. GU22: Wok 7J 5
Dorin Ct. GU22: Pyr 3B 12
Dorking Rd. GU1: Guild 3B 30
Dorking Vs. GU21: Knap 1K 9
Dormers Cl. GU7: G'mng 7K 27
Dorrit Cres. GU3: Guild 2A 22
Dorset Dr. GU21: Wok 4K 11
Dorset Way KT14: Byfl 1H 7
Dorton Way GU23: Rip 5F 13
Douglas Cl. GU4: Jac W 5F 17
Douglas Dr. GU7: G'mng 2B 34
Dovedale Cl. GU4: Burp 1J 23

Dover Ct.—Fullerton Rd.

Dover Ct. GU6: Cranl 5F 37
Doverfield Rd. GU4: Burp 1J 23
Doversmead GU21: Knap 7A 4
Downer Mdw. GU7: G'mng 6A 28
Downhurst Rd. GU6: Ewh 2K 37
Downing Av. GU2: Guild 5B 22
Down La. GU3: Comp, Guild 3H 27
Down Rd. GU1: Guild 4K 23
Downs Dr. GU1: Guild 4A 24
Downsedge Ter. GU1: Guild 4K 23
Downside Orchard GU22: Wok 1J 11
Downside Rd. GU4: Guild 5K 23
Downsview Av. GU22: Wok 5H 11
Downsview Ct. GU1: Guild 7E 16
Downsway GU1: Guild 4C 24
Drakes Cl. GU6: Cranl 5D 36
Drakes Way GU22: Wok 6F 11
Dray Ct. GU2: Guild 5D 22
Drive, The GU2: Guild 4B 22
(Beech Gro.)
GU2: Guild 6B 22
(The Crossways)
GU3: Art 1D 28
GU5: Wone 1K 35
GU6: Cranl 6D 36
GU7: Eash 3E 32
GU7: G'mng 5A 34
GU8: P Har 3E 32
GU22: Wok 4D 10
Drodges Cl. GU5: Bram 6H 29
Drove Rd. GU4: Guild 6D 24
GU5: Shere 6J 25
Drummond Ct.
GU1: Guild 2C 38 (4F 23)
Drummond Rd.
GU1: Guild 2C 38 (4F 23)
Duchess of Kent Cl. GU2: Guild . . . 7D 16
Dukes Cl. GU6: Cranl 6F 37
Dukes Ct. GU21: Wok 1H 11
Duke's Dr. GU7: G'mng 7H 27
Duke St. GU21: Wok 1H 11
Duncan Dr. GU1: Guild 3J 23
Duncombe Rd. GU7: G'mng 5K 33
Dunfee Way KT14: Byfl 3J 7
Dunlin Ri. GU4: Guild 2B 24
Dunmore GU2: Guild 3K 21
Dunmow Ho. KT14: Byfl 4J 7
Dunnets GU21: Knap 1A 10
DUNSBOROUGH PARK 5G 13
Dunsdon Av. GU2: Guild 5D 22
Dunstall Grn. GU24: Chob 1E 4
Durham Cl. GU2: Guild 2B 22
Durnsford Way GU6: Cranl 6E 36
Dykes Path GU21: Wok 6A 6
Dynevor Pl. GU3: Worp 7J 15

E

Eagle Rd. GU1: Guild 2D 38 (4F 23)
EASHING 3F 33
Eashing La. GU7: Eash 3F 33
GU8: Mil 5F 33
Easington Pl. GU1: Guild 5H 23
Eastbrook Cl. GU21: Wok 7J 5
Eastbury La. GU3: Comp 3G 27
EAST CLANDON 1H 25
Eastcroft Ct. GU1: Guild 5J 23
E. Flexford La. GU3: Wanb 6F 21
East Gdns. GU22: Wok 1A 12
Eastgate GU22: Wok 1H 11
Eastgate Ct. GU1: Guild . . . 4D 38 (5F 23)
Eastgate Gdns.
GU1: Guild 3E 38 (5G 23)
East Hill GU22: Wok 7A 6
Eastmead GU21: Wok 1D 10
East Meads GU2: Guild 5B 22
EAST SHALFORD 3J 29
E. Shalford La. GU4: Guild 2G 29
East Vw. Cotts. *GU6: Cranl 5B 36*
(off East Vw. La.)
East Vw. La. GU6: Cranl 5B 36
East Way GU2: Guild 4B 22
Eastwood Lodge GU5: Bram 7H 29
Eastwood Rd. GU5: Bram 7H 29
Eaton Ct. GU1: Guild 2J 23
Eaton Ho. *GU1: Guild 6H 23*
(off St Lukes Sq.)
Ebbage Ct. GU22: Wok 2G 11
Echo Pit Rd. GU1: Guild 1G 29
Ecob Cl. GU3: Guild 7B 16
Eden Cl. KT15: New H 1F 7
Edencroft GU5: Bram 7H 29
Eden Gro. Rd. KT14: Byfl 4J 7
Edgeborough Ct. GU1: Guild 5H 23
Edgefield Cl. GU6: Cranl 4B 36
Edgeley Cvn. Pk. GU5: Alb 6J 31
Edison Ho. *GU7: G'mng 3A 34*
(off Flambard Way)
Edward II Av. KT14: Byfl 5K 7
Edward Ho. GU1: Guild . . . 2D 38 (4F 23)
Effingham Ct. *GU22: Wok 3G 11*
(off Constitution Hill)
Egerton Ct. GU2: Guild 4A 22
Egerton Rd. GU2: Guild 4A 22
Egley Dr. GU22: Wok 6F 11
Egley Rd. GU22: Wok 6F 11
Elcho Rd. GU24: Brkwd 3C 8
Elder Cl. GU4: Burp 1J 23
Elder Rd. GU24: Bisl 6G 3
Eleanor Ct. GU1: Guild . . . 5D 38 (6F 23)
Electric Theatre
Guildford 4B 38 (5E 22)
Elgin Gdns. GU1: Guild 3J 23
Elizabeth Ct. GU7: G'mng 7A 28
Elizabeth Rd. GU7: G'mng 7A 28
Elkins Gdns. GU4: Burp 1J 23
Ellery Cl. GU6: Cranl 7D 36
Elles Av. GU1: Guild 4A 24
Ellingham GU22: Wok 3G 11
Ellis Av. GU2: Guild 6B 22
Ellis Farm Cl. GU22: Wok 6F 11
Elmbank Av. GU2: Guild 5C 22
Elmbridge Cotts. GU6: Cranl 5A 36
Elmbridge Est. GU22: Wok 3H 11
Elmbridge La. GU22: Wok 3H 11
Elmbridge Rd. GU6: Cranl 5A 36
Elm Cl. GU21: Wok 6F 5
GU23: Rip 1E 18
Elm Ct. GU21: Knap 1K 9
Elmcroft *GU22: Wok 2H 11*
(off Fairview Av.)
Elmdene Ct. *GU22: Wok 3G 11*
(off Constitution Hill)
Elmdon Pl. GU1: Guild 3H 23
Elm Dr. GU24: Chob 1B 4
Elm Fld. Cotts. GU3: Woo V 3G 21
Elmfield Ho. GU4: Guild 2A 24
Elm Gro. GU24: Bisl 7G 3
Elmgrove Cl. GU21: Wok 3K 9
Elmgrove La. GU3: Norm 1C 20
ELM HILL 1A 20
Elmhurst Ct. GU1: Guild 5H 23
Elm La. GU23: Ock 3K 13
Elm Pk. GU6: Cranl 5A 36
Elm Rd. GU7: G'mng 6B 28
GU21: Wok 6H 5
(Heath Rd.)
GU21: Wok 2F 11
(The Mount)
Elmside GU2: Guild 5C 22
GU8: Mil 6F 33
Elmstead Rd. KT14: W Byf 4E 6
Elmtree Cl. KT14: Byfl 4J 7
Elmwood Rd. GU21: Wok 3K 9
Elphinstone Cl. GU24: Brkwd 5F 9
Elsdon Rd. GU21: Wok 2C 10
Elstead Rd. GU8: Shack 1C 32
Elveden Cl. GU22: Pyr 1F 13
Elveden Pl. GU22: Pyr 1F 13
Ely Pl. GU2: Guild 2B 22
Emmanuel Cl. GU2: Guild 1C 22
Emmetts Cl. GU21: Wok 1F 11
Englefield Rd. GU21: Knap 1J 9
Engliff La. GU22: Pyr 7E 6
Ennismore Av. GU1: Guild 4H 23
Enterprise Est. GU1: Guild 7G 17
Envis Way GU3: Worp 7J 15
Epsom Pl. GU6: Cranl 5E 36
Epsom Rd. GU1: Guild . . . 4E 38 (5G 23)
(not continuous)
GU4: E Clan, Guild, W Cla . . . 3C 24
KT24: W Hor 1J 25
Erica Cl. GU24: W End 4E 2
Erica Ct. GU22: Wok 2F 11
Escombe Dr. GU2: Guild 6D 16
Eurobet Ho. *GU21: Wok 1G 11*
(off Church St. W.)
Europa Pk. Rd. GU1: Guild 3E 22
Eustace Rd. GU4: Guild 2B 24
Evelyn Cl. GU22: Wok 4F 11
Everest Ct. GU21: Wok 7A 4
Everlands Cl. GU22: Wok 2G 11
Eve Rd. GU21: Wok 6K 5
Eversleigh Flats *GU1: Guild 4H 23*
(off Buckingham Cl.)
EWHURST 3K 37
EWHURST GREEN 4K 37
Ewhurst Rd. GU6: Cranl 5D 36
Exchange, The *GU22: Wok 1H 11*
(off Oriental Rd.)
Exeter Pl. GU2: Guild 2B 22
Eyston Dr. KT13: Weyb 1K 7

F

Fairborne Way GU2: Guild 1C 22
Fairbourne Cl. GU21: Wok 2C 10
Fairfax Rd. GU22: Wok 4K 11
Fairfield Cl. GU2: Guild 3C 22
Fairfield La. GU24: W End 3G 3
Fairfield Lodge *GU2: Guild 3C 22*
(off Fairfield Ri.)
Fairfield Ri. GU2: Guild 3B 22
Fairford Cl. KT14: W Byf 5D 6
FAIRLANDS 7J 15
Fairlands Av. GU3: Worp 7J 15
Fairlands Ct. GU3: Worp 7J 15
Fairlands Rd. GU3: Worp 6J 15
Fairlawn Pk. GU21: Wok 5G 5
Fairlawns GU1: Guild 4A 24
KT15: Wdhm 2D 6
Fairmead GU21: Wok 2E 10
Fairoaks Cvn. Pk. GU3: Worp 6G 15
Fairview Av. GU22: Wok 2G 11
Fairview Cl. GU22: Wok 2H 11
Fairwater Dr. KT15: New H 1H 7
Fairway GU1: Guild 3B 24
Fairway, The GU3: Worp 1J 15
GU7: G'mng 5B 34
KT13: Weyb 2K 7
Fairway Cl. GU22: Wok 3D 10
Falcon Cl. GU18: Light 2A 2
Falcon Ct. GU21: Wok 4A 6
Falcon Rd. GU1: Guild . . . 3D 38 (5F 23)
(not continuous)
Falstone GU21: Wok 2D 10
Faraday Rd. GU1: Guild . . . 1B 38 (3E 22)
Faris Barn Dr. KT15: Wdhm 3D 6
Faris La. KT15: Wdhm 2D 6
Farleigh Ct. GU2: Guild 4A 22
Farleigh Rd. KT15: New H 2E 6
FARLEY GREEN 6H 31
FARLEY HEATH 7G 31
Farley Heath Rd.
GU5: Sha G, Alb 7G 31
Farm Cl. GU1: Guild 1F 23
GU3: Worp 6J 15
KT14: Byfl 3K 7
Farmhouse Cl. GU22: Pyr 6B 6
Farm La. GU23: Send 1A 18
Farm Rd. GU22: Wok 4K 11
Farm Wlk. GU2: Guild 6B 22
FARNCOMBE 7A 28
Farncombe Boat House 1C 34
Farncombe Hill GU7: G'mng 7K 27
Farncombe Station (Rail) 7B 28
Farncombe St. GU7: G'mng 7A 28
Farnham Rd.
GU1: Guild 5A 38 (7K 21)
GU2: Guild 5A 38 (7K 21)
FARNHAM ROAD HOSPITAL
. . . . . 5A 38 (6D 22)
Farnley GU21: Wok 1B 10
Farriers, The GU5: Bram 2J 35
Farthingham La. GU6: Ewh 2K 37
Farthings GU21: Knap 7A 4
Fawley Cl. GU6: Cranl 6E 36
Fays Pas. GU1: Guild . . . 4B 38 (5E 22)
Felix Dr. GU4: W Cla 5E 18
Fellow Grn. GU24: W End 4F 3
Fellow Grn. Rd. GU24: W End 4F 3
Fennel Cl. GU1: Guild 1K 23
Fennscombe Ct. GU24: W End 4E 2
Fenns La. GU24: W End 4E 2
Fenns Way GU21: Wok 6G 5
Fentum Rd. GU2: Guild 2C 22
Fenwick Cl. GU21: Wok 2D 10
Ferndale GU3: Guild 2A 22
Ferndale Rd. GU21: Wok 7H 5
Fernden Ri. GU7: G'mng 7A 28
Ferndown Cl. GU1: Guild 5J 23
Ferndown Ct. GU1: Guild 3E 22
Ferney Ct. KT14: Byfl 2H 7
Ferney Rd. KT14: Byfl 3H 7
Fernhill Cl. GU22: Wok 4E 10
Fernhill La. GU22: Wok 4E 10
Fernhill Pk. GU22: Wok 4E 10
Fernihough Cl. KT13: Weyb 1K 7
Fernley Ho. GU7: G'mng 6A 28
Fern Mead GU6: Cranl 5G 37
Fern Rd. GU7: G'mng 1B 34
Ferry La. GU2: Guild 1E 28
Fettes Rd. GU6: Cranl 5F 37
Field Cl. GU4: Guild 2B 24
Field End GU24: W End 4F 3
Fielders Grn. GU1: Guild 4J 23
Fieldings, The GU21: Wok 7B 4
Field La. GU7: G'mng 7B 28
Field Pl. GU7: G'mng 7A 28
Field Vw. Cotts. GU7: G'mng 3H 33
Field Way GU23: Rip 2D 18
Filmer Gro. GU7: G'mng 2A 34
Finch Cl. GU21: Knap 1J 9
Finches Ri. GU1: Guild 2K 23
Finch Rd. GU1: Guild . . . 2D 38 (4F 23)
Findlay Dr. GU3: Guild 7B 16
Firbank Dr. GU21: Wok 3D 10
Firbank La. GU21: Wok 3D 10
Fircroft Cl. GU22: Wok 2H 11
Fircroft Ct. GU22: Wok 2H 11
Firgrove GU21: Wok 3D 10
Firs, The GU3: Art 1D 28
GU24: Bisl 7G 3
KT14: Byfl 3H 7
Firs Av. GU5: Bram 1J 35
Firsway GU2: Guild 3B 22
Fir Tree Rd. GU1: Guild 1E 22
Firwood Cl. GU21: Wok 3A 10
Fisher Rowe Cl. GU5: Bram 1J 35
Fitzjohn Cl. GU4: Guild 1A 24
Five Oaks Cl. GU21: Wok 3K 9
Flambard Way GU7: G'mng 3K 33
Fleetwood Ct. KT14: W Byf 4E 6
Fletcher Cl. *GU21: Wok 2B 10*
(off Robin Hood Rd.)
FLEXFORD 4B 20
Flexford Rd. GU3: Flex 5B 20
Flexlands La. GU24: Chob 1H 3
Flitwick Grange GU8: Mil 6F 33
Florence Av. KT15: New H 2E 6
Florence Ct. GU21: Knap 2J 9
Florence Way GU21: Knap 2J 9
Florida Rd. GU4: Shalf 3G 29
Flower Wlk. GU2: Guild . . . 7B 38 (7E 22)
Floyd's La. GU22: Pyr 7E 6
Folly, The GU18: Light 3B 2
Forbench Cl. GU23: Rip 6F 13
Ford Rd. GU22: Wok 4K 11
GU24: Bisl, W End 5E 2
GU24: Chob 1J 3
Forest Cl. GU22: Pyr 6B 6
Foresters Cl. GU21: Wok 2B 10
Forest Rd. GU22: Pyr 6B 6
Forge End GU21: Wok 1G 11
Forster Rd. GU2: Guild 7C 16
Forsythia Pl. GU1: Guild 2E 22
Forsyth Path GU21: Wok 4B 6
Forsyth Rd. GU21: Wok 6A 6
Fort Rd. GU1: Guild 7E 38 (7G 23)
Fortune Dr. GU6: Cranl 7D 36
Fosse Way KT14: W Byf 4D 6
Fosters La. GU21: Knap 1J 9
Foundation Units GU1: Guild 7G 17
Four Acres GU1: Guild 2A 24
Fowlers Cft. GU3: Comp 4H 27
Fowlers Mead GU24: Chob 1A 4
Foxburrow Hill GU5: Bram 7F 29
Foxburrow Hill Rd. GU5: Bram . . . 7F 29
Foxburrows Av. GU2: Guild 4B 22
Foxburrows Ct. GU2: Guild 3B 22
Fox Cl. GU22: Pyr 6B 6
FOX CORNER 2J 15
Fox Corner Community Wildlife Area
. . . . . 2J 15
Fox Covert GU18: Light 2A 2
Fox Dene GU7: G'mng 5J 33
Foxenden Rd.
GU1: Guild 3E 38 (5G 23)
Foxes Path GU4: Sut G 3H 17
Foxglove Gdns. GU4: Guild 2A 24
Foxgrove Dr. GU21: Wok 6J 5
Foxhanger Gdns. GU22: Wok 7J 5
Foxhills GU21: Wok 1E 10
Foxlake Rd. KT14: Byfl 3K 7
Foxleigh Grange GU24: Bisl 1H 9
Frailey Cl. GU22: Wok 7K 5
Frailey Hill GU22: Wok 7K 5
Francis Ct. GU2: Guild 2D 22
Francis Crick Rd. GU2: Guild 5K 21
Franklin Ct. *GU2: Guild 4B 22*
(off Derby Rd.)
Franklyn Rd. GU7: G'mng 4H 33
Franks Rd. GU2: Guild 1C 22
Frederick Sanger Rd.
GU2: Guild 5K 21
Freesia Dr. GU24: Bisl 7G 3
Fremantle Way GU24: Brkwd 3D 8
French's Wells GU21: Wok 1D 10
Freshborough Ct. GU1: Guild 5H 23
Friars Cft. GU4: Guild 1A 24
Friar's Ga. GU2: Guild 6C 22
Friars Ri. GU22: Wok 2J 11
Friary, The GU1: Guild . . . 4B 38 (5E 22)
Friary Bri. GU1: Guild . . . 5B 38 (6E 22)
Friary Ct. GU21: Wok 2B 10
Friary Pas. GU1: Guild . . . 5B 38 (6E 22)
Friary St. GU1: Guild . . . 5B 38 (6F 23)
FRITH HILL 1K 33
Frith Hill Rd. GU7: G'mng 7K 27
Frobisher Gdns. GU1: Guild 3J 23
Frog Gro. La. GU3: Woo V 2F 21
Frog La. GU4: Sut G 2G 17
Fuchsia Way GU24: W End 4E 2
Fulbrook Av. KT15: New H 2E 6
Fullbrook School Sports Cen. 3E 6
Fullerton Cl. KT14: Byfl 5K 7
Fullerton Dr. KT14: Byfl 5J 7
Fullerton Rd. KT14: Byfl 5J 7

A-Z Guildford & Woking 43

Fullerton Way—Heathside Gdns.

Fullerton Way KT14: Byfl 5J 7
Fullmer Way KT15: Wdhm 1D 6
Furlough, The GU22: Wok 7J 5
Furtherfield GU6: Cranl 4D 36
Furzehill Cotts. GU24: Pirb 6C 8
Furze La. GU7: G'mng 6B 28

G

Gables, The GU2: Guild 1D 22
Gables Cl. GU22: Wok 4H 11
Gables Ct. GU22: Wok 4H 11
Gadbridge La. GU6: Ewh 4K 37
Gala Bingo
Woking *1H 11*
(within The Big Apple)
Gale Dr. GU18: Light 1A 2
Gales Cl. GU4: Guild 1B 24
Galvins Cl. GU2: Guild 1C 22
Gambles La. GU23: Rip 1G 19
Ganghill GU1: Guild 2J 23
Gapemouth Rd. GU24: Pirb 6A 8
Gardenia Dr. GU24: W End 4F 3
Gardens, The GU24: Pirb 6F 9
Gardner Rd. GU1: Guild . . . 1C 38 (4F 23)
Gate St. GU5: Bram 6J 35
(not continuous)
Gateway, The GU21: Wok 5K 5
Gateways GU1: Guild 4J 23
Gatley Dr. GU4: Burp 1H 23
GATWICK 1A 32
Gaveston Cl. KT14: Byfl 4K 7
Genesis Bus. Pk. GU21: Wok 6A 6
Genyn Rd. GU2: Guild 4A 38 (5D 22)
Georgelands GU23: Rip 5F 13
George Rd. GU1: Guild . . 2C 38 (4F 23)
GU7: G'mng 7A 28
GU8: Mil 5F 33
George St. GU24: Brkwd 5A 8
Germander Dr. GU24: Bisl 6G 3
Gibb's Acre GU24: Pirb 7F 9
Giffard Way GU2: Guild 1C 22
Gill Av. GU2: Guild 5A 22
Gilliat Dr. GU4: Guild 2B 24
Gingers Cl. GU6: Cranl 6E 36
Girdlestoneites GU7: G'mng 7J 27
Glade, The KT14: W Byf 4C 6
Glade M. GU1: Guild 5H 23
Glaziers La. GU3: Flex, Norm 2B 20
Glebe, The GU6: Ewh 2K 37
Glebe Cl. GU18: Light 1C 2
Glebe Cotts. GU4: W Cla 2F 25
Glebe Ct. GU1: Guild 4H 23
Glebe Gdns. KT14: Byfl 5H 7
Glebe Rd. GU6: Cranl 5C 36
Glen Ct. GU21: Wok 3C 10
KT14: Byfl 2H 7
Glendale Cl. GU21: Wok 2E 10
Glendale Dr. GU4: Burp 1A 24
Glenlee GU22: Wok 3E 10
G Live
Guildford 3E 38 (5G 23)
Gloster Ct. *GU21: Wok 7H 5*
(off Walton Rd.)
Gloster Rd. GU22: Wok 4J 11
Gloucester Rd. GU2: Guild 2B 22
Gloucester Sq. GU21: Wok 1G 11
Gloucester Wlk. GU21: Wok 1G 11
GODALMING 3A 34
Godalming Bus. Cen.
GU7: G'mng 3B 34
Godalming Leisure Cen. 7C 28
Godalming Mus. 3K 33
Godalming Station (Rail) 3K 33
Goddard Cl. GU2: Guild 7C 16
Godley Rd. KT14: Byfl 5K 7
Goldfinch Gdns. GU4: Guild 3B 24
Goldfort Wlk. GU21: Knap 7A 4
Goldings, The GU21: Wok 7B 4
Goldsmiths Cl. GU21: Wok 2E 10
GOLDSWORTH 2F 11
Goldsworth Orchard
GU21: Wok 2C 10
GOLDSWORTH PARK 1C 10
Goldsworth Pk. Cen., The
GU21: Wok 1C 10
Goldsworth Pk. Trad. Est.
GU21: Wok 7C 4
Goldsworth Rd. GU21: Wok 2E 10
Goldsworth Rd. Ind. Est.
GU21: Wok 1F 11
Goldvale Ho. *GU21: Wok 1G 11*
(off Church St. W.)
Gole Rd. GU24: Pirb 5C 8
Golf Cl. GU22: Pyr 5C 6
Golf Club Rd. GU22: Wok 4C 10
Goose La. GU22: Wok 6D 10
Goose Rye Rd. GU3: Worp 3K 15
Gorse Bank GU18: Light 3A 2
Gorse Ct. GU4: Guild 2A 24
Gorse Hill GU22: Wok 5B 10
Gorselands Cl. KT14: W Byf 2G 7
Gorsewood Rd. GU21: Wok 3K 9
Gosden Cl. GU5: Bram 6H 29
GOSDEN COMMON 6G 29
Gosden Comn. GU5: Bram 7G 29
Gosden Cotts. GU5: Bram 7H 29
Gosden Hill Rd. GU4: Burp 7A 18
Gosden Rd. GU24: W End 4F 3
Gould Ct. GU4: Guild 2B 24
Gownboys GU7: G'mng 7J 27
GRAFHAM 7K 35
Grafton Cl. KT14: W Byf 4D 6
Grandis Cotts. GU23: Rip 6F 13
Grange, The GU2: Guild 1D 22
GU24: Chob 1A 4
Grange Cl. GU2: Guild 7D 16
GU7: G'mng 2C 34
Grange Dr. GU21: Wok 6G 5
Grangefields Rd. GU4: Jac W 5F 17
Grange Pk. GU6: Cranl 5E 36
GU21: Wok 6G 5
Grange Rd. GU2: Guild 6D 16
GU21: Wok 5G 5
GU24: Pirb 6C 8
KT15: New H 1E 6
Gransden Cl. GU6: Ewh 3K 37
Grantley Av. GU5: Wone 1K 35
Grantley Cl. GU4: Shalf 4G 29
Grantley Gdns. GU2: Guild 3C 22
Grantley Rd. GU2: Guild 3C 22
Granville Cl. KT14: Byfl 4K 7
Granville Rd. GU22: Wok 4H 11
Grasmere Cl. GU1: Guild 3K 23
Grasmere Rd. GU18: Light 1B 2
Grasmere Way KT14: Byfl 3K 7
Gravetts La. GU3: Guild 1K 21
Graylands GU21: Wok 7G 5
Graylands Cl. GU21: Wok 7G 5
Graylands Ct. GU1: Guild 5H 23
Grayling Cl. GU7: G'mng 5K 33
Grays Rd. GU7: G'mng 7B 28
Greatford Dr. GU1: Guild 4B 24
Gt. George St. GU7: G'mng 3A 34
Gt. Goodwin Dr. GU1: Guild 2K 23
Gt. Oaks Pk. GU4: Burp 6K 17
Great Quarry
GU1: Guild 7D 38 (7F 23)
Great Tangley GU5: Wone 5K 29
Green, The GU6: Ewh 3K 37
GU23: Rip 5G 13
Greenacre GU21: Knap 7A 4
Greenbush La. GU6: Cranl 7E 36
Greencroft GU1: Guild 4K 23
Green Dr. GU23: Rip 7D 12
Greenham Wlk. GU21: Wok 2E 10
Greenheys Pl. GU22: Wok 2H 11
Greenhill Cl. GU7: G'mng 4K 33
Greenhill Gdns. GU4: Guild 2A 24
Green La. GU1: Guild 4K 23
GU3: Woo V 2G 21
GU4: W Cla 4E 18
GU5: Alb, Sha G 7E 30
GU7: G'mng 5K 27
GU8: Mil 7E 32
GU22: Wok 5D 10
GU24: Chob 1B 4
KT14: Byfl 3K 7
Green La. Cl. KT14: Byfl 3K 7
Green La. E. GU3: Flex 5A 20
Greenmeads GU22: Wok 6G 11
Greenside Cl. GU4: Guild 2A 24
Greenside Cotts. GU23: Rip 5G 13
Greenvale Rd. GU21: Knap 2K 9
Greenway Cl. KT14: W Byf 4E 6
Greenwood, The GU1: Guild 3J 23
Greenwood Cl. KT15: Wdhm 2D 6
Greenwood Rd. GU21: Wok 4A 10
GU24: Brkwd 5B 8
Gregory Cl. GU21: Wok 1E 10
Grenville Rd. GU8: Shack 7D 26
Gresham Ho. GU22: Wok 6J 11
Gresham Pk. Rd. GU22: Wok 5K 11
Greville Cl. GU2: Guild 4A 22
Greyfriars Dr. GU24: Bisl 6G 3
Greyfriars Rd. GU23: Rip 1E 18
Greylees GU7: G'mng 2A 34
Greythorne Rd. GU21: Wok 2C 10
Greywaters Dr. GU5: Bram 1J 35
Grindstone Cres. GU21: Knap 2H 9
GRINDSTONE HANDLE CORNER . . . 2H 9
Grobars Av. GU21: Wok 6E 4
Groom Wlk. GU1: Guild 1G 23
Grosvenor Ct. GU4: Burp 1K 23
Grosvenor Ho. GU1: Guild 5H 23
Grosvenor Pl. *GU21: Wok 1H 11*
(off Stanley Rd.)
Grosvenor Rd. GU7: G'mng 4A 34
GU24: Chob 4K 3
Grove, The GU21: Wok 7H 5
Grove Cl. GU6: Cranl 7E 36
GROVE HEATH 7F 13
Gro. Heath Ct. GU23: Rip 1G 19
Gro. Heath Nth. GU23: Rip 6F 13
Gro. Heath Rd. GU23: Rip 7F 13
Grove Rd. GU1: Guild 4A 24
GU6: Cranl 7E 36
GU7: G'mng 4J 33
GU21: Wok 7H 5
Grovers Farm Cotts.
KT15: Wdhm 2C 6
Guernsey Cl. GU4: Burp 6J 17
Guernsey Farm Dr.
GU21: Wok 6F 5
Guildcroft GU1: Guild 4J 23
GUILDFORD 5C 38 (4C 22)
Guildford & Godalming By-Pass Rd.
GU2: Guild 7F 27
GU3: Comp, Guild 7F 27
GU8: Mil, P Har, Shack 6E 32
Guildford Boat House 6C 38 (6F 23)
Guildford Bus. Pk. GU2: Guild 3D 22
Guildford Bus. Pk. Rd.
GU2: Guild 3D 22
Guildford Bus Station 4B 38 (5E 22)
Guildford Castle 5C 38 (6F 23)
Guildford Cathedral 4C 22
Guildford Ct. GU2: Guild 4C 22
Guildford Crematorium
GU7: G'mng 6D 28
Guildford Golf Course 5A 24
Guildford Guildhall & House Gallery
. . . . . 4D 38 (5F 23)
Guildford Ind. Est. GU2: Guild 4C 22
Guildford La. GU5: Alb 7C 24
GU22: Wok 3F 11
Guildford Lido 3F 23
Guildford Mus. 5C 38 (6F 23)
GUILDFORD NUFFIELD
HEALTH HOSPITAL 4A 22
GUILDFORD PARK 5D 22
Guildford Pk. Av.
GU2: Guild 3A 38 (5D 22)
Guildford Pk. Rd.
GU2: Guild 4A 38 (5D 22)
Guildford Rd. GU3: Norm 1A 20
GU3: Worp 7F 9
GU4: Sut G 4F 17
GU6: Cranl 1A 36
GU7: G'mng 7C 28
GU18: Light 1A 2
GU21: Knap 5F 3
GU21: Wok 2K 5
GU22: Wok 6F 11
(Bourne Way)
GU22: Wok 3G 11
(Wych Hill La.)
GU24: Bisl, W End 3E 2
GU24: Chob 5K 3
GU24: Pirb 7F 9
KT16: Ott 2K 5
Guildford Station
(Rail) 4A 38 (5E 22)
Guildown Av.
GU2: Guild 7A 38 (7D 22)
Guildown Rd.
GU2: Guild 7B 38 (7D 22)
Guildway, The GU3: Art 3E 28
Guileshill La. GU23: Ock 7J 13
Guinness Ct. GU21: Wok 2B 10
Gumbrells Cl. GU3: Worp 7J 15
Gwynne Ct. *GU2: Guild 7D 16*
(off Grange Rd.)

H

Hacketts La. GU22: Pyr 5D 6
Hailey Pl. GU6: Cranl 4E 36
Halebourne La.
GU24: Chob, W End 1G 3
Hale Ends GU22: Wok 5D 10
Half Moon Cotts. GU23: Rip 5G 13
Halfpenny Cl. GU4: Guild 3B 30
Halfpenny La. GU4: Guild 6A 24
Halfway La. GU7: Eash 3G 33
Hallam Rd. GU7: G'mng 1B 34
Hall Cl. GU7: G'mng 7A 28
Hall Dene Cl. GU1: Guild 3A 24
Halley's App. GU21: Wok 1C 10
Halley's Ct. GU21: Wok 2C 10
Hallington Cl. GU21: Wok 1D 10
Hallowes Cl. GU2: Guild 6D 16
Hall Pl. GU21: Wok 7J 5
Hall Rd. GU5: Bram 1H 35
Halls Farm Cl. GU21: Knap 1K 9
Hamble Cl. GU21: Wok 1C 10
Hambledon Rd. GU7: Bus 5B 34
GU8: Bus 7B 34
Hamble Wlk. GU21: Wok 2C 10
Hamilton Av. GU22: Pyr 6C 6
Hamilton Cl. GU2: Guild 6C 16
Hamilton Dr. GU2: Guild 6C 16
Hamilton Gordon Ct.
GU1: Guild 3E 22
Hamilton Pl. GU2: Guild 6C 16
KT14: W Byf 4D 6
Hammond Cl. GU21: Wok 6E 4
Hammond Rd. GU21: Wok 6E 4
Hammond Way GU18: Light 1B 2
Hampton Cl. GU21: Knap 3J 9
Hanbury Path GU21: Wok 5B 6
Hanger Ct. GU21: Knap 1A 10
Hannah Gdns. GU2: Guild 2C 22
Hanover Ct. GU1: Guild 2F 23
GU22: Wok 3G 11
Hanson Cl. GU4: Burp 1H 23
Harcourt Cotts. GU3: Putt 2C 26
Hare Hill Cl. GU22: Pyr 6E 6
Harelands Cl. GU21: Wok 1E 10
Harelands La. GU21: Wok 2E 10
(not continuous)
Hare La. GU7: G'mng 1B 34
Hareward Rd. GU4: Guild 2A 24
Harms Gro. GU4: Guild 1A 24
Harrier Cl. GU6: Cranl 4D 36
Harrowdene GU6: Cranl 4D 36
Harrow La. GU7: G'mng 7A 28
Hartland Cl. KT15: New H 1G 7
Hart Rd. KT14: Byfl 4J 7
Harts Gdns. GU2: Guild 1D 22
Harts Hill GU2: Guild 3K 21
Hartshill Wlk. GU21: Wok 7D 4
Harts Yd. GU7: G'mng 3A 34
Harvest Hill GU7: G'mng 3K 33
Harvey Gallery
Guildford 5E 38 (6G 23)
Harvey Gdns. *GU1: Guild 6G 23*
(off Addison Rd.)
Harvey Lodge *GU1: Guild 5G 23*
(off Harvey Rd.)
Harvey Rd. GU1: Guild . . 5E 38 (6G 23)
Hascombe Rd. GU8: Bus 6C 34
Haskells Yd. *GU7: G'mng 3A 34*
(off Wharf St.)
Haslemere Rd. GU8: Mil 7E 32
Hassall Ct. GU22: Wok 5J 11
Hatchingtan, The GU3: Worp 3E 16
HATCHLANDS 1K 25
Hatchlands Pk. 7K 19
Hatfield Cl. KT14: W Byf 3F 7
Hawkswell Cl. GU21: Wok 1B 10
Hawkswell Wlk. GU21: Wok 1B 10
Hawthorn Cl. GU22: Wok 4G 11
Hawthorne Way GU4: Burp 7K 17
Hawthorn Pl. GU4: Guild 2B 24
Hawthorn Rd. GU7: G'mng 5H 33
GU22: Wok 4F 11
GU23: Rip 1E 18
Hawthorn Way GU24: Bisl 7G 3
KT15: New H 1G 7
Hayden Ct. KT15: New H 2F 7
Haydon Pl. GU1: Guild . . . 3C 38 (5F 23)
Hayes Barton GU22: Pyr 7B 6
Haynes Cl. GU23: Rip 6F 13
Hazel Av. GU1: Guild 7E 16
Hazel Ct. GU1: Guild 7F 17
Hazel Dr. GU23: Rip 2D 18
Hazelhurst Cl. GU4: Burp 6K 17
Hazel Rd. KT14: W Byf 5E 6
Hazelwood Cotts. GU7: G'mng . . . 3K 33
Hazelwood Rd. GU21: Knap 2A 10
Heath, The GU3: Putt 2D 26
Heathdown Rd. GU22: Pyr 6B 6
Heath Dr. GU23: Send 6K 11
GU24: Brkwd 4G 9
Heather Cl. GU2: Guild 3D 22
GU21: Wok 6E 4
KT15: New H 1F 7
Heatherfields KT15: New H 1F 7
Heathervale Cvn. Pk.
KT15: New H 1G 7
Heathervale Rd. KT15: New H 1F 7
Heathervale Way KT15: New H 1G 7
Heather Wlk. GU24: Brkwd 5D 8
Heathfield Cl. GU7: G'mng 5A 34
GU22: Wok 2J 11
Heathfield Rd. GU22: Wok 2J 11
Heath Ho. Rd. GU22: Wok 6J 9
Heathlands Cl. GU21: Wok 5G 5
Heathlands Vis. Cen. 1A 2
Heath La. GU5: Alb 4J 31
GU7: Bus 5C 34
Heath M. GU23: Rip 7F 13
Heath Mill La. GU3: Worp 2H 15
Heath Ri. GU23: Rip 7F 13
Heath Rd. GU21: Wok 6H 5
Heathside Cres. GU22: Wok 1H 11
Heathside Gdns. GU22: Wok 1J 11

44 A-Z Guildford & Woking

Heathside Pk. Rd. GU22: Wok 2H 11
Heathside Rd. GU22: Wok 2H 11
Hedgecroft Cotts. GU23: Rip 6H 19
Hedgerley Ct. GU21: Wok 1E 10
Hedgers Almshouses
  GU1: Guild 3B 24
    (off Wykeham Rd.)
Hedgeway GU2: Guild 6C 22
Heights, The KT13: Weyb 1K 7
Helford M. GU7: G'mng 6B 28
Helford Wlk. GU21: Wok 2C 10
Helmsdale GU21: Wok 2D 10
Hemsley Cl. GU2: Guild 1C 22
Henage La. GU22: Wok 4A 12
Henchley Dene GU4: Guild 7D 16
Henderson Av. GU2: Guild 7D 16
Henley Bank GU2: Guild 6C 22
Henley Bus. Pk. GU3: Norm 6C 14
Henley Cl. GU22: Wok 4K 11
Henley Fort Bungs. GU2: Guild . . .7C 22
Henley Fort
  (Surrey Outdoor
    Learning Development) 7C 22
Henley Ga. GU3: Norm 4C 14
  GU24: Pirb 4C 14
Henley Pk. GU3: Norm 6C 14
Hennessy Cl. GU22: Wok 4A 6
Henslow Way GU21: Wok 5B 6
Herbert Cres. GU21: Knap 2A 10
Hereford Cl. GU2: Guild 2B 22
Hereford Copse GU22: Wok 3D 10
Hermitage Bri. GU21: Wok 4K 9
Hermitage Bri. Cotts.
  GU21: Wok 3J 9
Hermitage Rd. GU21: Wok 3K 9
Hermitage Woods Cres.
  GU21: Wok 1A 26
Hermitage Woods Est.
  GU21: Wok 4K 9
Heron Cl. GU2: Guild 1D 22
Heronscourt GU18: Light 2C 2
Heron Shaw GU6: Cranl 7D 36
Herons Way GU24: Brkwd 5D 8
Heron Wlk. GU21: Wok 5A 6
Hesketh Cl. GU6: Cranl 5D 36
Hewitts Ind. Est. GU6: Cranl 5A 36
Heythorp Cl. GU21: Wok 1B 10
Heywood GU7: G'mng 7J 27
Hidcote Cl. GU22: Wok 7K 5
HIGH CLANDON 3J 25
Highclere Cl. GU2: Guild 2J 23
Highclere Ct. GU21: Knap 1J 9
Highclere Gdns. GU21: Knap 1J 9
Highclere Rd. GU21: Knap 1J 9
Highcotts La. GU4: W Cla 3D 18
Highcroft GU8: Mil 7E 32
Highdene GU22: Wok 2H 11
    (off Fairview Av.)
Highfield GU4: Shalf 5H 29
Highfield Cl. KT14: W Byf 4E 6
Highfield Ho. GU7: G'mng 3A 34
Highfield La. GU3: Putt 3A 26
Highfield Rd. KT14: W Byf 4E 6
High Gdns. GU22: Wok 3D 10
Highgrove Ho. GU4: Guild 2A 24
Highlands La. GU22: Wok 5G 11
High Path Rd. GU1: Guild 4A 24
High Pewley
  GU1: Guild 6E 38 (6G 23)
High Ridge GU7: G'mng 5J 33
High Rd. KT14: Byfl 3H 7
High St. GU1: Guild 5C 38 (6F 23)
  GU2: Guild 5B 38 (6E 22)
  GU5: Bram 1H 35
  GU6: Cranl 5B 36
  GU7: G'mng 3K 33
  GU21: Knap 1J 9
  GU22: Wok 1H 11
    (Commercial Way)
  GU21: Wok 6D 4
    (Horsell Birch)
  GU22: Wok 5J 11
  GU23: Rip 5G 13
  GU24: Chob 2A 4
  GU4: W End 3F 3
Highview GU21: Knap 1A 10
High Vw. Rd. GU2: Guild 7K 21
Hilgay GU1: Guild 4H 23
Hilgay Cl. GU1: Guild 4H 23
Hilgay Rd. GU1: Guild 4H 23
Hilibrow Cl. GU3: Woo V 3H 21
Hill Cl. GU5: Wone 1K 35
  GU7: G'mng 7F 5
Hill Ct. GU7: G'mng 7A 28
Hillcrest Ho. GU4: Guild 2A 24
Hillcrest Rd. GU2: Guild 3B 22
Hillfield Cl. GU1: Guild 2A 24
Hilliards Vw. GU6: Cranl 3D 36
Hillier Ho. GU2: Guild 6D 22

Hillier Rd. GU1: Guild 4J 23
Hillmount GU22: Wok 2G 11
    (off Constitution Hill)
Hillside GU22: Wok 4F 11
Hillside Cl. GU21: Knap 1K 9
Hillside Ct. GU1: Guild 5G 23
Hillside Wlk. GU1: Guild 2A 38 (4E 22)
Hillside Way GU7: G'mng 7K 27
Hillspur Cl. GU2: Guild 3B 22
Hillspur Rd. GU2: Guild 3B 22
Hilltop Cl. GU3: Guild 7B 16
Hill Vw. Ct. GU22: Wok 2H 11
Hill Vw. Cres. GU2: Guild 2B 22
Hill Vw. Rd. GU22: Wok 2H 11
Hipley Cl. GU1: Guild 5J 23
Hipley St. GU22: Wok 4K 11
Hitherbury Cl.
  GU2: Guild 7B 38 (7E 22)
Hitherwood GU6: Cranl 6D 36
HMP Coldingley GU24: Bisl 1F 9
HMP Send GU23: Send 4G 19
Hoad Cres. GU22: Wok 6H 11
Hobbs Cl. KT14: W Byf 4F 7
Hockering Est. GU22: Wok 2J 11
Hockering Gdns. GU22: Wok 2J 11
Hockering Rd. GU22: Wok 2J 11
Hockford Cl. GU24: Pirb 3H 15
Hodgson Gdns. GU4: Burp 1J 23
Hodgsonites GU7: G'mng 7H 27
Hoebridge Golf Course 3A 12
Hoebrook Cl. GU22: Wok 5H 11
Hoe Ct. GU22: Wok 3G 11
Hogan Bus. Cen. GU21: Wok 1G 11
Hog's Back GU2: Guild 7A 38 (7K 21)
  GU3: Comp, Guild, Putt, Wanb
    .1A 26
Holbreck Pl. GU22: Wok 2H 11
Holbrook Cl. GU4: Shalf 5G 29
Holford Rd. GU1: Guild 4A 24
Hollands, The GU22: Wok 2G 11
Hollies Av. KT14: W Byf 4D 6
Hollow, The GU7: Eash 3F 33
HOLLOWAY HILL 5A 34
Holloway Hill GU7: G'mng 3K 33
Hollow Cl. GU2: Guild 5D 22
Holly Av. KT15: New H 1E 6
Hollybank GU4: W End 4F 3
Holly Bank Rd. GU22: Wok 5D 10
Hollybank Rd. KT14: W Byf 5E 6
Hollybush La. GU23: Rip 3H 13
Holly Cl. GU21: Wok 3D 10
Hollyhock Dr. GU24: Bisl 6G 3
Holly La. GU3: Worp 6J 15
  GU7: G'mng 3J 33
Holly Lea GU4: Jac W 5F 17
Holly Lodge GU22: Wok 1H 11
    (off Heathside Cres.)
Holm Cl. KT15: Wdhm 3C 6
Holm Ct. GU7: G'mng 7K 27
Holmefield Pl. KT15: New H 1F 7
Holmes Cl. GU22: Wok 5H 11
Holmesdale Cl. GU1: Guild 3K 23
Holyoake Av. GU21: Wok 1E 10
Holyoake Cres. GU21: Wok 1E 10
Homebeech Ho. GU22: Wok 2G 11
    (off Mt. Hermon Rd.)
Home Farm Cotts. GU8: P Har 2C 32
Home Farm Rd. GU7: Bus 5A 34
Homefield Cl. KT15: Wdhm 3C 6
Home Pk. Cl. GU5: Bram 1H 35
Homestall GU2: Guild 4K 21
Homestead GU6: Cranl 4E 36
Homestead Dr. GU3: Norm 1D 20
Home Vs. GU5: Alb 6G 31
Homewood GU6: Cranl 5F 37
Homeworth Ho. GU22: Wok 2G 11
    (off Ashdown Cl.)
Honeypots Rd. GU22: Wok 4D 10
HOOK HEATH 4D 10
Hook Heath Av. GU22: Wok 3D 10
Hook Heath Gdns. GU22: Wok 5B 10
Hook Heath Rd. GU22: Wok 5D 10
Hook Hill La. GU22: Wok 5D 10
Hook Hill Pk. GU22: Wok 5D 10
Hook La. GU3: Putt 2C 26
  GU24: W End 4C 2
Hook Mill La. GU18: Light 1D 2
Hookstone La. GU24: W End 2F 3
Hopfield GU21: Wok 7G 5
Hopfield Av. KT14: Byfl 3J 7
Hopkin Cl. GU2: Guild 7D 16
Hopton Ct. GU2: Guild 4A 22
    (off Park Barn Dr.)
Horizon Bus. Village
  KT13: Weyb 3K 7
Hornbeam Rd. GU1: Guild 1E 22
Hornhatch GU4: Guild 3K 29
Hornhatch Cl. GU4: Guild 3K 29
Hornhatch La. GU4: Guild 3J 29
Horseblock Hollow GU6: Cranl 1F 37

HORSELL 7E 4
Horsell Birch GU21: Wok 6C 4
HORSELL COMMON 2J 5
Horsell Comn. Rd. GU21: Wok 5E 4
Horsell Moor GU21: Wok 1F 11
Horsell Pk. GU21: Wok 7F 5
Horsell Pk. Cl. GU21: Wok 7F 5
Horsell Ri. GU21: Wok 6F 5
Horsell Ri. Cl. GU21: Wok 6F 5
Horsell Va. GU21: Wok 7G 5
Horsell Way GU21: Wok 7E 4
Horseshoe, The GU7: G'mng 4J 33
Horseshoe La. GU6: Cranl 4B 36
Horseshoe La. E. GU1: Guild 3K 23
Horseshoe La. W. GU1: Guild 3K 23
Horsham Rd. GU4: Shalf 5F 29
  GU5: Bram 5F 29
  GU6: Cranl 6D 36
Howard Cl. GU21: Knap 3J 9
    (off Tudor Way)
Howard Gdns. GU1: Guild 3J 23
Howard Ridge GU4: Burp 7J 17
Howards Cl. GU22: Wok 4J 11
Howards Rd. GU22: Wok 4H 11
Hudson Ct. GU2: Guild 4B 22
Humbolt Cl. GU2: Guild 4B 22
Hungry Hill La.
  GU23: Rip, Send 3G 19
Hunter Rd. GU1: Guild 5G 23
Huntingdon Rd. GU21: Wok 1B 10
Hunts Cl. GU2: Guild 3K 21
Hunts Ct. GU2: Guild 1B 20
HUNTS HILL 1B 20
Hunts Hill Rd. GU3: Norm 7A 14
Hurley Gdns. GU4: Burp 1J 23
Hurlford GU21: Wok 1C 10
Hurst Cl. GU22: Wok 4E 10
Hurst Cft. GU1: Guild 7G 23
Hurst Farm Cl. GU8: Mil 5F 33
Hurst Hill Cotts. GU5: Bram 2J 35
Hurst Way GU22: Pyr 5C 6
HURTMORE 7F 27
HURTMORE BOTTOM 1F 33
Hurtmore Chase GU7: Hurt 7H 27
Hurtmore Golf Course 7F 27
Hurtmore Rd. GU7: Hurt, G'mng . . .7F 27
Hurtwood La. GU5: Alb, Shere 7J 31
Huxley Cl. GU7: G'mng 7K 27
Huxley Rd. GU2: Guild 5K 21

I

Ilex Ho. KT15: New H 1E 6
Inglehurst KT15: New H 1F 7
Inglewood GU21: Wok 2D 10
Inkerman Rd. GU21: Knap 2A 10
Inkerman Way GU21: Wok 2A 10
Inwood Cl. GU22: Wok 6H 11
Iris Dr. GU24: Bisl 6G 3
Iris Rd. GU24: Bisl 6G 3
Iron La. GU5: Bram 2F 35
Irwin Rd. GU2: Guild 5C 22
Iveagh Rd. GU2: Guild 5D 22
Ivor Cl. GU1: Guild 5H 23
Ivybank GU7: G'mng 1A 34
Ivydene GU21: Knap 2H 9
Ivy Dr. GU18: Light 3A 2
Ivy La. GU22: Wok 1K 11

J

Jackmans La. GU21: Wok 3C 10
JACOBS WELL 5F 17
Jacob's Well Rd. GU4: Jac W 6F 17
James Black Rd. GU2: Guild 5K 21
James Rd. GU3: Peasm 5E 28
Janoway Hill La. GU21: Wok 3E 10
Japonica Cl. GU21: Wok 2E 10
Jasmine Cl. GU21: Wok 7B 4
Jasons Dr. GU4: Guild 1A 24
Jefferson Rd. GU24: Brkwd 4C 8
Jeffries Pas.
  GU1: Guild 4D 38 (5F 23)
Jenner Dr. GU24: W End 4G 3
Jenner Rd. GU1: Guild 4E 38 (5G 23)
Jersey Cl. GU4: Burp 6K 17
John Norman Gro. GU18: Light 1B 2
John Russell Cl. GU2: Guild 1C 22
Johnston Grn. GU2: Guild 7C 16
Johnston Wlk. GU2: Guild 7C 16
John Wiskar Dr. GU6: Cranl 5C 36
Jolive Ct. GU1: Guild 5J 23
Jordans Cl. GU1: Guild 5J 23
Joseph's Rd. GU1: Guild 3F 23
Jubilee Sq. GU21: Wok 1G 11
    (off Church St. E.)
Julian Cl. GU21: Wok 2B 10
Junction Rd. GU18: Light 1B 2
Junewood Cl. KT15: Wdhm 2D 6

Juniper Cl. GU1: Guild 6D 16
Juniper Dr. GU24: Bisl 6G 3
Juniper Pl. GU4: Shalf 4F 29

K

Kalima Cvn. Site GU24: Chob 1D 4
Katana GU22: Wok 3G 11
    (off Brooklyn Rd.)
Katherine Ct. GU21: Knap 3J 9
    (off Tudor Way)
Kaye Don Way KT13: Weyb 1K 7
Keens La. GU3: Guild 7B 16
Keens Pk. Rd. GU3: Guild 7B 16
Keepers Cl. GU4: Guild 1B 24
Kemishford GU22: Wok 7C 10
Kenton Way GU21: Wok 1B 10
Kentwell Cl. GU2: Guild 7K 5
Kenworth Gro. GU18: Light 1A 2
Kernel Ct.
  GU1: Guild 1A 38 (4E 22)
Kerria Way GU24: W End 4E 2
Kerry Ter. GU21: Wok 7K 5
Kersland Cotts. GU7: Hurt 7F 27
Kestrel Cl. GU4: Guild 2B 24
Kestrel Ho. GU2: Guild 6D 4
Keswick Dr. GU18: Light 2B 2
Kettlewell Cl. GU21: Wok 5F 5
Kettlewell Dr. GU21: Wok 5G 5
Kettlewell Hill GU21: Wok 5G 5
Kevan Dr. GU23: Send 1C 18
Killicks GU6: Cranl 4E 36
Kiln Copse GU6: Cranl 4D 36
Kiln La. GU23: Rip 1E 18
  GU24: Bisl 1H 9
Kiln Mdws. GU3: Worp 7J 15
Kilrush Ter. GU21: Wok 7J 5
Kimber Ct. GU21: Wok 2B 24
Kingcup Dr. GU24: Bisl 6G 3
KINGFIELD 4J 11
Kingfield Cl. GU22: Wok 4H 11
Kingfield Dr. GU22: Wok 4H 11
Kingfield Gdns. GU22: Wok 4H 11
KINGFIELD GREEN 4H 11
Kingfield Grn.
  GU22: Wok 4H 11
Kingfield Rd. GU22: Wok 4G 11
Kingfield Stadium 4H 11
Kingfisher Ct. GU2: Guild 2B 24
  GU22: Wok 1G 11
    (off Vale Farm Rd.)
  GU21: Wok 5A 6
    (Woodlands Pk.)
Kingfisher Dr. GU4: Guild 2A 24
King George's Dr.
  KT15: New H 1E 6
Kinglake Cl. GU21: Wok 2A 10
Kingpost Pde. GU1: Burp 1K 23
King's Av. GU24: Brkwd 3D 8
Kings Av. KT14: Byfl 3H 7
Kings Cl. KT14: Byfl 2H 7
Kingsdowne Rd. GU7: G'mng 1B 34
Kingsfield GU5: Alb 7J 31
Kings Ga. GU7: G'mng 1B 34
    (off King's Rd.)
Kingshead La. KT14: Byfl 2H 7
Kingsmead GU6: Cranl 5D 36
  GU21: Wok 7J 5
Kings M. GU4: Shalf 3G 29
Kingsmoor Pk. GU22: Wok 6H 11
Kingsoak Ho. GU21: Wok 5A 6
King's Rd. GU1: Guild 2D 38 (4F 23)
  GU7: G'mng 1B 34
  Kings Rd. GU4: Shalf 4G 29
  GU6: Cranl 6D 36
  GU21: Wok 7J 5
  GU24: W End 5G 3
  KT15: New H 1F 7
Kingston La. GU4: W Hor 4K 19
Kingston Ri. KT15: New H 1E 6
Kingsway GU21: Wok 2F 11
Kingsway Av. GU21: Wok 2F 11
Kingsway Bus. Pk. GU21: Wok 5A 6
Kingswood Ct. GU21: Wok 3A 24
Kingswood Ct. GU22: Wok 7G 5
Kings Yd. GU2: Guild 1B 22
Kirby Rd. GU21: Wok 1E 10
Kirkfields GU2: Guild 1C 22
Kirkland Av. GU21: Wok 7A 4
KNAPHILL 1K 9
Knightsbridge Ho. GU1: Guild 5H 23
    (off St Lukes Sq.)
Knightswood GU21: Wok 2B 10
Knoll Quarry GU7: G'mng 1A 34
Knoll Rd. GU7: G'mng 1K 33
Knoll Wood GU7: G'mng 1K 33
Knowle Gdns. KT14: W Byf 4D 6
Knowle La. GU6: Cranl 6C 36

Knowl Hill GU22: Wok 3K 11
Knox Rd. GU2: Guild 6C 16
Kyngeshene Gdns. GU1: Guild 5K 23

L

Laburnum Cl. GU1: Guild 1E 22
Laburnum Rd. GU22: Wok 4F 11
Ladycross GU8: Mil 7E 32
Ladygrove Dr. GU4: Burp 6J 17
Ladymead GU1: Guild 3E 22
Ladymead Retail Cen.
  GU1: Guild 3E 22
LA Fitness
  Goldsworth 1F 11
  Guildford 3C 24
Lake Cl. KT14: Byfl 3H 7
Lakes Cl. GU4: Guild 3K 29
Lakeside GU21: Wok 3A 10
Lakeside Cl. GU21: Wok 3A 10
Lakeside Dr. GU24: Chob 4A 4
Laleham Ct. GU21: Wok 7G 5
Lambourne Cres. GU21: Wok 4B 6
Lammas Cl. GU7: G'mng 1C 34
Lammas Ct. GU7: G'mng 2A 34
  (off Old Station App.)
Lammas Rd. GU7: G'mng 2C 34
Lampeter Cl. GU22: Wok 2G 11
Lancaster Av. GU1: Guild 6H 23
Lancaster Cl. GU21: Wok 7J 5
Lane End Dr. GU21: Knap 1J 9
Langdale Cl. GU21: Wok 7E 4
Langham Cl. GU7: G'mng 2B 34
Langham Pk. GU7: G'mng 2B 34
Langley Cl. GU1: Guild 3E 22
Langley Pl. GU2: Guild 7C 16
Langley Wlk. GU22: Wok 3G 11
Langmans Cl. GU21: Wok 2D 10
Langmans Way GU21: Wok 7A 4
Langshott Cl. KT15: Wdhm 2C 6
Langton Cl. GU21: Wok 1B 10
Lansbury Est. GU21: Knap 2K 9
Lansdown Cl. GU21: Wok 4J 23
Lansdown Cl. GU21: Wok 3B 10
Lapwing Gro. GU4: Guild 2B 24
Larch Av. GU1: Guild 2E 22
Larches, The GU21: Wok 7G 5
Larchwood Rd. GU21: Wok 4K 9
Larkfield GU6: Ewh 4K 37
Larks Way GU21: Wok 7J 3
Lascombe La. GU3: Putt 2A 26
Laserquest
  Woking 1H 11
  (within The Big Apple)
Lashmere GU6: Cranl 5A 36
Latimer Cl. GU22: Wok 7K 5
Latimer Rd. GU7: G'mng 3A 34
Laundry Rd. GU1: Guild 3B 38 (5E 22)
  (off Bagshot Rd.)
Laurel Bank GU24: Chob 2A 4
Laurel Cres. GU21: Wok 4A 6
Laureldene GU3: Flex 4B 20
Laurel Gdns. KT15: New H 1F 7
Lauriston Cl. GU21: Knap 1K 9
Laustan Cl. GU1: Guild 4A 24
Lavender Pk. Rd. KT14: W Byf 3E 6
Lavender Rd. GU22: Wok 7K 5
Lawford's Hill Cl. GU3: Worp 1J 15
Lawford's Hill Rd. GU3: Worp 1J 15
Lawn Rd. GU2: Guild 7B 38 (7E 22)
Lawns, The GU8: Mil 6F 33
Lawnsmead GU5: Wone 7K 29
Lawnsmead Cotts. GU5: Wone 7K 29
Lawnwood Cotts. GU7: G'mng 2C 34
  (off Catteshall La.)
Lawrence Cl. GU4: Burp 6K 17
Leafield Cl. GU21: Wok 2E 10
Leapale La. GU1: Guild 4C 38 (5F 23)
Leapale Rd. GU1: Guild 3B 38 (5E 22)
Lea's Rd. GU1: Guild 3B 38 (5E 22)
Ledger Cl. GU1: Guild 2K 23
Leegate Cl. GU21: Wok 7D 4
Leehurst GU8: Mil 6E 32
Leisure La. KT14: W Byf 7F 7
Leslie Rd. GU24: Chob 1A 4
Levylsdene GU1: Guild 4A 24
Levylsdene Ct. GU1: Guild 4B 24
Lewis Elton Gallery 4C 22
Leybourne Av. KT14: Byfl 4K 7
Leybourne Cl. KT14: Byfl 4K 7
Liddington Hall Dr. GU3: Guild 1A 22
Liddington New Rd. GU3: Guild . . .1A 22
Lido Rd. GU1: Guild 3E 23
Lidstone Cl. GU21: Wok 1D 10
Lightbox Mus., The 7G 5
LIGHTWATER 1B 2
Lightwater By-Pass GU18: Light . . .1A 2
Lightwater Mdw. GU18: Light 2B 2
Lightwater Rd. GU18: Light 2B 2

Lilac Av. GU22: Wok 4F 11
Lilac Cl. GU1: Guild 7E 16
Lilyfields Chase GU6: Ewh 4K 37
Limebush Cl. KT15: New H 1G 7
Lime Cl. GU4: W Cla 5F 19
Limecroft Rd. GU21: Knap 1H 9
Lime Gro. GU1: Guild 7D 16
  GU4: W Cla 5E 18
  GU22: Wok 5G 11
Lime Quarry M. GU1: Guild 3B 24
Limes, The GU21: Wok 7J 5
  (off Maybury Rd.)
  GU21: Wok 6F 5
  (Ridgeway)
Lime Tree Wlk. GU21: Wok 7F 5
Lime Wlk. GU5: Shere 2K 31
Limewood Cl. GU21: Wok 4K 9
Lincoln Dr. GU22: Pyr 6C 6
Lincoln Rd. GU2: Guild 2B 22
Linden Cl. KT15: New H 2E 6
Linden Rd. GU1: Guild 1C 38 (4F 23)
Linden Way GU22: Wok 5H 11
  GU23: Rip 2D 18
Lindfield Gdns. GU1: Guild 3H 23
Lindsay Rd. KT15: New H 1E 6
Lindvale GU21: Wok 6G 5
Linersh Dr. GU5: Bram 1J 35
Linersh Wood GU5: Bram 1J 35
Linersh Wood Cl. GU5: Bram 2J 35
Ling Dr. GU18: Light 3A 2
Link Av. GU22: Pyr 6B 6
Links Bus. Cen. GU21: Wok 3A 12
Links Cl. GU6: Ewh 3J 37
Links Rd. GU5: Bram 7G 29
Linkway GU21: Guild 3B 22
  GU22: Wok 1A 12
Linnet Gro. GU4: Guild 2B 24
Lion Retail Pk. GU22: Wok 7K 5
Lipcombe Cotts. GU5: Alb 6G 31
Liquorice La. GU4: Guild 6H 11
Litchfield Way GU2: Guild 6B 22
Littlefield Cl. GU3: Worp 7K 15
LITTLEFIELD COMMON 6K 15
Littlefield Way GU3: Worp 7J 15
Littleford La. GU4: Blckh 5C 30
  GU5: Sha G 5C 30
Little Hide GU1: Guild 3H 23
Little Kiln GU7: G'mng 6A 28
LITTLE LONDON 4K 31
Little London GU5: Alb 4J 31
Little Mnr. Gdns. GU6: Cranl 6D 36
Little Mead GU6: Cranl 6A 36
Littlemead GU21: Wok 7B 4
Littlemoor Gdns. GU22: Wok 1A 12
Lit. Moreton Cl. KT14: W Byf 3F 7
Little Orchard GU21: Wok 5J 5
  KT15: Wdhm 2E 6
Lit. Orchard Way GU4: Shalf 4G 29
Little Platt GU2: Guild 3K 21
Little Riding GU22: Wok 7K 5
Little Thatch GU7: G'mng 1B 34
LITTLETON 2C 28
Littleton La. GU3: Art 2C 28
Lit. Tumners Ct. GU7: G'mng 7A 28
Lit. Warren Cl. GU4: Guild 6K 23
LITTLEWICK 7A 4
LITTLEWICK COMMON 6A 4
Littlewick Rd. GU21: Knap, Wok . . .7A 4
Littlewood GU6: Cranl 5E 36
Livingstone Rd. GU21: Wok 7F 36
Llanaway Cl. GU7: G'mng 1B 34
Llanaway Ho. GU7: G'mng 1B 34
  (off Meadrow)
Llanaway Rd. GU7: G'mng 1B 34
Lobelia Rd. GU24: Bisl 6G 3
Lock Cl. KT15: Wdhm 3C 6
Locke Way GU21: Wok 1H 11
Lockfield Dr. GU21: Wok 7A 4
Lockhurst Hatch La. GU5: Alb 7J 31
Lockites GU7: G'mng 7J 27
  (off Queen's Dr.)
Lock La. GU22: Pyr 7F 7
LOCKNER HOLT 3D 30
Lock Rd. GU1: Guild 1F 23
Locksley Dr. GU21: Wok 1B 10
Lockswood GU24: Brkwd 4H 9
Lockwood Path GU21: Wok 4B 6
Loder Cl. GU21: Wok 4B 6
Lombard St. GU8: Shack 1A 32
Lombardy Cl. GU21: Wok 1B 10
Loncin Mead Av. KT15: New H 1G 7
London Rd. GU1: Guild 3E 38 (3G 23)
  GU4: Burp 7K 17
  (not continuous)
  GU23: Send 3C 18
London Rd. Station
  (Rail) 2E 38 (4G 23)
London Sq. GU1: Guild 4G 23

Longbourne Grn. GU7: G'mng 6A 28
Longdown Rd. GU4: Guild 7K 23
Long Dyke GU1: Guild 3H 23
Long Gore GU7: G'mng 5A 28
Long Ho's. GU24: Pirb 1D 14
Longmead GU1: Guild 4A 24
Longpoles Rd. GU6: Cranl 6E 36
Longridge Gro. GU22: Pyr 5D 6
Longs Cl. GU22: Pyr 7E 6
Long Wlk. GU4: E Clan 7J 19
  GU1: W Byf 5G 7
Loop Rd. GU22: Wok 4H 11
LORDSHILL COMMON 3K 35
Loretto Cl. GU6: Cranl 5E 36
Lorne Gdns. GU21: Knap 3K 9
Loseley Pk. 3A 28
Loseley Rd. GU7: G'mng 6A 28
Lothian Rd. GU24: Brkwd 5A 8
Louis Flds. GU3: Worp 7J 15
Loveday Ho. GU6: Cranl 3B 36
Lovelace Dr. GU22: Pyr 7C 6
Lovelands La. GU24: Chob 4J 3
Lovells Cl. GU18: Light 1B 2
LOWER EASHING 3F 33
Lower Eashing GU7: Eash 3E 32
Lwr. Edgeborough Rd.
  GU1: Guild 5H 23
Lwr. Guildford Rd. GU21: Knap 1K 9
Lwr. Manor Rd. GU7: G'mng 1A 34
  GU8: Mil 6E 32
Lwr. Moushill La. GU8: Mil 6D 32
Lwr. Pyrford Rd. GU22: Pyr 7F 7
Lower Sandfields GU23: Send 1B 18
Lower Sth. St. GU7: G'mng 3K 33
Lower St. GU5: Shere 2K 31
Lowfield Cl. GU18: Light 2A 2
Lowthorpe GU21: Wok 2C 10
Loxley Cl. KT14: Byfl 5J 7
LUCAS GREEN 6D 2
Lucas Grn. Rd. GU24: W End 6D 2
Lucerne Cl. GU22: Wok 3G 11
Ludlow Rd. GU2: Guild 4A 38 (5D 22)
Lych Way GU21: Wok 7F 5
Lydele Cl. GU21: Wok 6H 5
Lydger Cl. GU22: Wok 4K 11
Lynchmere Pl. GU2: Guild 1C 22
Lyndale Cl. KT14: W Byf 4E 6
Lyndhurst Cl. GU21: Wok 6F 5
Lynton Ho. GU22: Wok 2G 11
  (off Station App.)
Lynwood Cl. GU21: Wok 5D 22
Lynwood Cl. GU21: Wok 4B 6
Lyons Dr. GU2: Guild 6C 16
Lytton Rd. GU22: Wok 7K 5

M

Mabel St. GU21: Wok 2F 11
McAlmont Ridge GU7: G'mng 7K 27
McClaren Technology Cen.
  . . . . .2J 5
Macdonald Rd. GU18: Light 3A 2
Macdowall Rd. GU2: Guild 6D 16
Macmahon Cl. GU24: Chob 1A 4
Madeira Cl. KT14: W Byf 4E 6
Madeira Cres. KT14: W Byf 4D 6
Madeira Rd. KT14: W Byf 4D 6
Madrid Rd. GU2: Guild 5D 22
Magdalen Cl. KT14: Byfl 5J 7
Magdalen Cres. KT14: Byfl 5J 7
Magistrates' Court
  Guildford 3B 38 (5E 22)
Magnolia Pl. GU1: Guild 1E 22
Mahonia Cl. GU24: W End 4F 3
Mainstone Cres. GU24: Brkwd 5D 8
Mainstone Rd. GU24: Bisl 7F 3
Maitland Cl. KT14: W Byf 4E 6
Malacca Farm GU4: W Cla 4F 19
Mall, The GU1: Guild 4B 38 (5D 22)
Mallards Way GU18: Light 2A 2
Mallow Cres. GU4: Burp 1K 23
Malthouse Ct. GU4: W End 3F 3
Malthouse La. GU3: Worp 1J 15
  GU24: Pirb 7H 9
  GU24: W End 4F 3
Malthouses, The GU6: Cranl 5D 36
Maltings, The KT14: Byfl 4K 7
Mandeville Cl. GU2: Guild 1C 22
Manfield Pk. GU6: Cranl 3A 36
Mangles Cl. GU1: Guild 3B 38 (5E 22)
Mangles Rd. GU1: Guild 2F 23
Mannings Hill GU6: Cranl 2C 36
Manor, The GU8: Mil 6F 33
Manor Cl. GU2: Pyr 1D 12
Manor Cres. GU2: Guild 2D 22
  GU24: Brkwd 4D 8
  KT14: Byfl 4K 7
Manor Dr. KT15: New H 1E 6
Manor Farm GU3: Wanb 7C 20

Mnr. Farm Cl. GU3: Norm 2B 20
Mnr. Farm Cotts. GU3: Wanb 7C 20
Manor Flds. GU8: Mil 5E 32
Manor Gdns. GU2: Guild 2D 22
Manor Gro. GU22: Pyr 7A 28
Manor Lea Cl. GU8: Mil 6E 32
Manor Lea Rd. GU8: Mil 5E 32
Manor Lodge GU2: Guild 2D 22
Manor Pk. Village GU2: Guild 5A 22
Manor Rd. GU2: Guild 2D 22
  GU21: Wok 7E 4
  GU23: Rip 7D 12
Manor Ter. GU7: G'mng 1B 34
Manor Way GU2: Guild 7A 22
  GU22: Wok 5K 11
Mansel Cl. GU2: Guild 6D 16
Manston Rd. GU4: Burp 7J 17
Manville Ct. GU4: Shalf 5G 29
Maori Rd. GU1: Guild 4H 23
Maple Cl. GU2: Guild 7E 4
Mapledrakes Cl. GU6: Ewh 3K 37
Mapledrakes Rd. GU6: Ewh 3K 37
Maple Dr. GU18: Light 2A 2
Maple Gro. GU1: Guild 2F 23
  GU22: Wok 5G 11
Maplehatch Cl. GU7: G'mng 5A 34
Maple Rd. GU23: Rip 1E 18
Marcus Ct. GU22: Wok 2H 11
Mareschal Rd.
  GU2: Guild 6A 38 (6E 22)
Maresfield Ho. GU4: Guild 3B 24
  (off Merrow St.)
Margaret Rd.
  GU1: Guild 3B 38 (5E 22)
Marigold Ct. GU1: Guild 1G 23
Marigold Dr. GU24: Bisl 6G 3
Mariners Dr. GU3: Norm 1B 20
Marjoram Cl. GU2: Guild 7C 16
Marjorie Fosters Way
  GU24: Brkwd 3D 8
Markenfield Rd.
  GU1: Guild 2C 38 (4F 23)
Markenhorn GU7: G'mng 7K 27
Market Sq. GU21: Wok 1G 11
Market St. GU1: Guild 4C 38 (5F 23)
Mark Way GU7: Hurt, G'mng 6H 27
Marlborough Rd. GU21: Wok 7J 5
Marlyns Cl. GU4: Burp 1J 23
Marlyns Dr. GU4: Burp 7J 17
Marshall Pde. GU22: Pyr 6D 6
Marshall Rd. GU7: G'mng 2A 34
Marshwood Rd. GU18: Light 2D 2
Marston Rd. GU21: Wok 1D 10
Martens Pl. GU7: G'mng 1A 34
Martindale Cl. GU4: Guild 2B 24
Martindale Rd. GU22: Wok 2C 10
Martin Rd. GU2: Guild 3A 24
Martins Cl. GU1: Guild 3A 24
Martinsyde GU22: Wok 1A 12
Martin Way GU21: Wok 2C 10
Martland Ind. Est. GU22: Wok 7C 10
Martyr Rd. GU1: Guild 4C 38 (5F 23)
Martyr's La. GU21: Wok 3K 5
Mary Va. GU7: G'mng 4H 33
Mary Rd. GU1: Guild 3B 38 (5E 22)
Mathon Ct. GU1: Guild 4H 23
Maxwell Dr. KT14: W Byf 2G 7
Maybourne Ri. GU22: Wok 1F 17
MAYBURY 7A 6
Maybury Est. GU22: Wok 7A 6
Maybury Hill GU22: Wok 7K 5
Maybury Rough GU22: Wok 1K 11
May Cl. GU7: G'mng 5H 33
Mayfield Av. KT15: New H 1F 7
Mayfield Cl. KT15: New H 1G 7
Mayfield Gdns. KT15: New H 1F 7
MAYFORD 6E 10
Mayford Cl. GU22: Wok 6F 11
Mayford Grn. GU22: Wok 6E 10
Mayford Meadows Local Nature Reserve
  . . . . .6F 11
Mayhurst Av. GU22: Wok 7A 6
Mayhurst Cl. GU22: Wok 7A 6
Mayhurst Cres. GU22: Wok 7A 6
Mayhurst M. GU22: Wok 7A 6
Maysfield Rd. GU23: Send 7B 12
Mays Gro. GU23: Send 7B 12
Maytree Cl. GU1: Guild 7E 16
Maytrees GU21: Knap 1J 9
Mead Cl. GU6: Cranl 6D 36
Mead Ct. GU21: Knap 7A 4
Meadow Bank GU1: Guild 2E 22
Meadowbank Rd. GU18: Light 1C 2
Meadow Cl. GU7: G'mng 7A 28
  GU8: Mil 6G 33
Meadow Cotts. GU24: W End 3F 3
Meadow Dr. GU23: Rip 7D 12

Meadow Ho. GU4: Guild 3B 24
(off Merrow St.)
Meadowlands GU4: Guild 7F 19
Meadow Ri. GU21: Knap 1J 9
Meadow Rd. GU4: Burp 7J 17
Meadows, The
GU2: Guild 7B 38 (7E 22)
Meadow Vw. GU22: Wok 5H 11
(not continuous)
Meadow Way GU24: W End 3F 3
Mead Rd. GU6: Cranl 5D 36
Meadrow GU7: G'mng 2B 34
Meadrow Ct. GU7: G'mng 1C 34
Meadside GU22: Wok 2H 11
(off Park Rd.)
Meads Rd. GU1: Guild 4K 23
Mead Way GU4: Burp 6A 18
Meadway Dr. GU21: Wok 7E 4
Medawar Rd. GU2: Guild 5K 21
Medhurst Cl. GU24: Chob 1B 4
Medieval Undercroft
Guildford 5C 38
Medlar Cl. GU1: Guild 2E 22
Melbury Cl. KT14: W Byf 5E 6
Mellersh Hill Rd. GU5: Wone 7K 28
Melville Ct. GU2: Guild . . .7B 38 (7E 22)
Merchants Wlk. GU21: Knap 1J 9
Mercia Wlk. GU1: Wok 1H 11
Merlin Cl. GU21: Wok 5A 6
Merrist Wood Golf Course 6H 15
Merrivale Gdns. GU21: Wok 1E 10
MERROW 3K 23
Merrow Bus. Pk. GU4: Guild 1B 24
Merrow Chase GU1: Guild 4A 24
Merrow Comn. Rd. GU4: Guild . . .1A 24
Merrow Copse GU1: Guild 3K 23
Merrow Ct. GU1: Guild 4B 24
Merrow Cft. GU1: Guild 3A 24
MERROW DOWNS 5B 24
Merrow
(Park & Ride) 3C 24
Merrow La. GU4: Burp, Guild 6A 18
Merrow Pl. GU4: Guild 2B 24
Merrow St. GU4: Guild 2B 24
Merrow Way GU1: Guild 3B 24
Merrow Woods GU1: Guild 4K 23
Mews, The GU1: Guild . . .3A 38 (5E 22)
Meyrick Cl. GU21: Knap 7A 4
Michael La. GU2: Guild 6D 16
Michelet Cl. GU18: Light 1B 2
Middleview Dr. GU3: Norm 1E 20
Middle Wlk. GU21: Wok 1G 11
Midhope Cl. GU22: Wok 3G 11
Midhope Gdns. GU22: Wok 3G 11
Midhope Rd. GU22: Wok 3G 10
Midleton Cl. GU8: Mil 5F 33
Midleton Ind. Est. E. GU2: Guild . .4D 22
Midleton Ind. Est. Rd.
GU2: Guild 3D 22
Midleton Rd. GU2: Guild 3D 22
Midsummer Wlk. GU21: Wok 7F 5
Milcombe Cl. GU21: Wok 2E 10
Mile Path GU22: Wok 5B 10
MILES GREEN 1F 9
Milestone Cl. GU23: Rip 6E 12
MILFORD 6F 33
Milford By-Pass Rd. GU8: Mil 7D 32
Milford Golf Course 6G 33
Milford Heath Rd. GU8: Mil 7E 32
Milford Ho. GU8: Mil 6G 33
Milford Lodge GU8: Mil 7F 33
Milford Rd. GU8: Els, Mil 4A 32
MILFORD SPECIALIST
REHABILITATION HOSPITAL
. . . . .7J 33
Milford Station (Rail) 7H 33
Milkhouse Ga.
GU1: Guild 5D 38 (6F 23)
Millan Cl. KT15: New H 1F 7
Millbrook GU1: Guild . . .5B 38 (6F 23)
(off Claremont Rd.)
Mill Cleave KT14: W Byf 3E 6
(off Claremont Rd.)
Millennium Cotts. GU5: Alb 2G 31
Miller Rd. GU4: Guild 1A 24
Milford GU21: Wok 1D 10
Mill La. GU1: Guild 5C 38 (6F 23)
GU3: Peasm 5E 28
GU4: Guild 2D 30
GU5: Bram 1H 35
GU7: G'mng 3K 33
GU23: Rip 3H 13
KT14: Byfl 1D 14
KT14: Byfl 3K 7
Millmead GU1: Guild . . .5B 38 (6E 22)
GU2: Guild 5B 38 (6E 22)
KT14: Byfl 3K 7
Millmead Ct.
GU2: Guild 6B 38 (6E 22)
Millmead Ter.
GU2: Guild 6B 38 (6E 22)

Mill Reach GU5: Guild 1D 30
Mill Rd. GU3: Peasm 5E 28
Milton Cl. GU3: Norm 1B 20
Miltons Cres. GU7: G'mng 5H 33
MIMBRIDGE 4C 4
Mincing La. GU24: Chob 1B 4
Minster Rd. GU7: G'mng 5A 34
Mint, The GU7: G'mng 3K 33
Mint St. GU7: G'mng 3K 33
Mint Wlk. GU21: Knap 1A 10
Mitchells Cl. GU4: Shalf 3G 29
Mitchells Row GU4: Shalf 4G 29
Mizens Railway 7K 3
Moat Lodge GU6: Cranl 5C 36
Model Cotts. GU24: Pirb 5D 8
Molloy Ct. GU21: Wok 7J 5
Molyneux Rd. GU7: G'mng 7B 28
Monks Gro. GU3: Comp 2E 26
Monro Dr. GU2: Guild 1C 22
Montague Cl. GU18: Light 1A 2
Montagu Pl. GU4: Shalf 3G 29
Montgomerie Dr. GU2: Guild 6C 16
Montgomery Rd. GU2: Guild 2G 11
Monument Bri. Ind. Est. E.
GU21: Wok 6K 5
Monument Bri. Ind. Est. W.
GU21: Wok 6J 5
Monument Bus. Cen.
GU21: Wok 7F 5
Monument Rd. GU21: Wok 5J 5
Monument Way E. GU21: Wok . . .6K 5
Monument Way W. GU21: Wok . . .6K 5
Moore Rd. Brkwd 5B 8
Moorfield Cen., The
GU1: Guild 7F 17
Moorfield Point GU1: Guild 7G 17
Moorfield Rd. GU1: Guild 7F 17
Moorholme GU22: Wok 3G 11
Moorings, The KT14: W Byf 4F 7
Moorlands, The GU22: Wok 5H 11
Moor La. GU22: Wok 6G 11
Morcote Cl. GU4: Shalf 4G 29
More Circ. GU7: G'mng 7A 28
More Rd. GU7: G'mng 7A 28
Morgan Cl. GU2: Guild 7B 16
Morton Cl. GU21: Wok 6E 4
Morton Rd. GU21: Wok 6F 5
Moss La. GU7: G'mng 3K 33
Mount, The GU2: Guild . . .7A 38 (6E 22)
GU6: Cranl 6D 36
GU6: Ewh 2K 37
GU21: Knap 3J 9
GU21: Wok 3C 10
(Elm Rd.)
GU21: Wok 3C 10
(St John's Hill)
MOUNT ALVERNIA BMI HOSPITAL
. . . . .6G 23
Mount Cl. GU6: Ewh 3K 37
GU21: Wok 5E 10
Mount Ct. GU2: Guild . . .5B 38 (6E 22)
MOUNT HERMON 3E 10
Mt. Hermon Cl. GU22: Wok 3F 11
Mt. Hermon Rd. GU22: Wok 3F 11
Mount Pl. GU2: Guild . . .5B 38 (6E 22)
Mt. Pleasant
GU2: Guild 6B 38 (6E 22)
Mt. Pleasant Cl. GU18: Light 1A 2
Mount Rd. GU6: Cranl 6D 36
GU22: Wok 5D 10
GU24: Chob 5D 4
Mountside GU2: Guild . . .6A 38 (6D 22)
Mt. Side Pl. GU2: Guild 2H 11
Moushill La. GU8: Mil 7E 32
Mowbray Av. KT14: Byfl 4J 7
Mower Pl. GU6: Cranl 4D 36
Moyne Ct. GU21: Wok 2B 10
Muirfield Rd. GU21: Wok 2C 10
Mulberry Cl. GU21: Wok 5G 5
Mulberry Ct. GU4: Guild 2B 24
Mulgrave Way GU21: Knap 2A 10
Munday's Boro GU3: Putt 2A 26
Munday's Boro Rd. GU3: Putt 2A 26
Munstead Heath Rd.
GU5: Bram 5C 34
GU8: Bus 5C 34
Munstead Pk. GU8: Bus 4E 34
Munstead Vw. GU3: Art 1D 28
Munstead Vw. Rd. GU5: Bram 2F 35
Murray Grn. GU21: Wok 5A 6
Murray's La. KT14: W Byf, Byfl . . .5H 7
Murtmead La. GU3: Putt 3A 26
Mylor Cl. GU21: Wok 5G 5
Myrtle Rd. GU18: Light 2B 2

N

Napier Ct. GU21: Wok 7G 5
Napier Gdns. GU1: Guild 3K 23

Napper Pl. GU6: Cranl 7D 36
Nasturtium Dr. GU24: Bisl 6G 3
National Rifle Association &
National Shooting Cen.
Headquarters 3D 8
(off Queen's Way)
National Rifle Association Mus. . . .3D 8
Nelson Gdns. GU1: Guild 3J 23
Nethercote Av. GU21: Wok 1B 10
Nether Mt. GU2: Guild 6D 22
Nettles Ter.
GU1: Guild 2C 38 (4F 23)
Newark Cl. GU4: Burp 6K 17
GU23: Rip 5E 12
Newark Cotts. GU23: Rip 5E 12
Newark La. GU22: Pyr 3D 12
GU23: Rip 3D 12
New Bridge Cotts. GU6: Cranl 5A 36
(off Elmbridge Rd.)
Newbridge Ct. GU6: Cranl 5A 36
New Coppice GU21: Wok 3A 10
New Cotts. GU24: Pirb 6D 8
New Cross Rd. GU2: Guild 2C 22
New England Hill GU24: W End . . .3D 2
New Ho. Farm La. GU3: Woo V . . .3J 21
New Inn La. GU4: Burp 7K 17
Newlands Av. GU22: Wok 5H 11
NEWLANDS CORNER 6E 24
Newlands Corner Vis. Cen. 6E 24
Newlands Cres. GU1: Guild 6H 23
Newlands Flats GU1: Guild 4H 23
(off Buckingham Cl.)
New La. GU4: Sut G 6G 11
New Pk. Rd. GU2: Cranl 5D 36
New Pond Rd. GU3: Art, Comp . . .4K 27
GU7: G'mng 4K 27
New Rd. GU4: E Clan 1J 25
GU4: Shalf, Guild 4K 29
GU5: Alb 2H 31
GU5: Wone 6K 29
GU8: Mil 6E 32
Newsham Rd. GU21: Wok 1B 10
New Vic. Ct. GU7: G'mng 1H 33
New Victoria Theatre
Woking 1G 11
New Way GU7: G'mng 3H 33
New Zealand Golf Course 3B 6
NHS WALK-IN CENTRE
WOKING 2H 11
(within Woking Community Hospital)
Nicholas Gdns. GU22: Pyr 7D 6
Nightingale Ct. GU21: Wok 2A 10
Nightingale Rd.
GU1: Guild 1D 38 (4F 23)
GU7: G'mng 2A 34
Nightingales GU6: Cranl 7D 36
Norfolk Farm Cl. GU22: Pyr 7B 6
Norfolk Farm Rd. GU22: Pyr 6B 6
Norley La. GU5: Sha G 2K 35
NORMANDY 1B 20
Normandy Bus. Pk.
GU3: Norm 5E 14
NORMANDY COMMON 1A 20
Normandy Comn. La.
GU3: Norm 1B 20
NORNEY 1E 32
Norney Gro. GU8: Shack 1E 32
Northbourne GU7: G'mng 6B 28
North Ct. GU7: G'mng 7H 27
Northdown La. GU1: Guild 7G 23
Northdowns GU6: Cranl 7D 36
North Dr. Brkwd 5C 8
Northfield GU4: Shalf 5G 29
GU18: Light 2B 2
Northfleet Lodge GU22: Wok 3G 11
North Ho. GU6: Cranl 3B 36
North Moors GU1: Guild 7G 17
NORTH MUNSTEAD 7D 34
Nth. Munstead La. GU7: Bus 6C 34
GU8: Bus 6C 34
North Rd. GU2: Guild 1D 22
GU21: Wok 7J 5
North St. GU1: Guild 4C 38 (5F 23)
GU7: G'mng 7A 28
Northway GU2: Guild 2C 22
GU7: G'mng 7H 27
Northwood Av. GU21: Knap 4K 15
Norton Cl. GU3: Worp 4K 15
Nottingham Cl. GU21: Wok 2B 10
Nottingham Ct. GU21: Wok 2B 10
(off Nottingham Cl.)
Nuffield Health
West Byfleet 5F 7
Nugent Rd. GU2: Guild 4K 21
Nursery Cl. GU21: Wok 7E 4
KT15: Wdhm 1D 6
Nursery Gdns. GU4: Guild 3K 29
Nursery Rd. GU7: G'mng 7B 28
GU21: Knap 1K 9
Nuthurst Av. GU6: Cranl 5D 36

Nuttall Gdns. GU6: Cranl 3D 36
Nutwood GU7: G'mng 1K 33
(off Frith Hill Rd.)

O

Oakbank GU22: Wok 3G 11
Oak Cl. GU6: Ewh 2K 37
GU7: G'mng 6A 28
Oak Cott. Cl. GU3: Woo V 3J 21
Oakcroft GU4: Guild 5D 6
Oakcroft Rd. KT14: W Byf 5D 6
Oakdene GU24: Chob 1B 4
Oakdene Pl. GU3: Peasm 5E 28
Oakdene Rd. GU3: Peasm 5E 28
GU23: Rip 4K 33
Oakfield GU21: Wok 1A 10
Oakfields GU3: Guild 2A 22
KT14: W Byf 5F 7
Oakford M. GU4: Shalf 3G 29
Oak Grange Rd. GU4: W Cla 6F 19
Oak Gro. GU6: Cranl 7E 36
Oak Hill GU3: Woo V 2H 21
GU4: Burp 6A 18
Oakhurst GU21: Wok 7F 5
GU24: Chob 1A 4
Oaklands GU6: Cranl 7C 36
GU4: Shalf 5G 29
Oaklands Cl. GU4: Shalf 5G 29
GU21: Wok 6H 11
Oak La. GU22: Wok 7K 5
Oakland Ct. GU2: Guild 3K 21
Oakleigh GU18: Light 2C 2
Oakley Dell GU4: Guild 2A 24
Oakley Ho. GU7: G'mng 6A 28
Oak Mead GU7: G'mng 6K 27
Oak Pk. KT14: W Byf 4C 6
Oakridge GU4: W End 4F 3
Oaks, The GU3: Norm 1E 20
KT14: W Byf 5E 6
Oaks GU1: Guild 1G 11
Oaks Way GU23: Rip 1E 18
Oak Tree Cl. GU4: Burp 6A 18
GU4: Jac W 5F 17
GU21: Knap 2H 9
Oak Tree Dr. GU1: Guild 7E 16
Oak Tree Gdns. GU1: Guild 1K 23
Oak Tree Rd. GU8: Mil 6E 32
GU21: Knap 2H 9
Oaktrees GU7: G'mng 1K 33
Oakway GU21: Wok 3A 10
Oakwood GU2: Guild 6C 16
Oakwood Ct. GU24: Bisl 7G 3
Oakwood Gdns. GU21: Knap 2G 9
Oakwood Rd. GU21: Wok 3A 10
Occam Cl. GU2: Guild 4K 21
Occam Rd. GU2: Guild 4K 21
Ockenden GU22: Wok 3G 11
(off Constitution Hill)
Ockenden Cl. GU22: Wok 2H 11
Ockenden Gdns. GU22: Wok 2H 11
Ockenden Rd. GU22: Wok 2H 11
Ockfields GU8: Mil 6F 33
Ockford Dr. GU7: G'mng 3K 33
Ockford Dr. GU7: G'mng 4J 33
OCKFORD RIDGE 4H 33
Ockford Ridge GU7: G'mng 4H 33
Ockford Rd. GU7: G'mng 4J 33
Ockham La. GU23: Ock 4J 13
Ockley Cl. GU4: Burp 6K 17
Ockley Rd. GU6: Ewh 2K 37
Odeon Cinema
Guildford 4B 38 (5E 22)
Off Up. Manor Rd. GU7: G'mng . . .7A 28
(off Up. Manor Rd.)
Oglethorpe Ct. GU7: G'mng 3K 33
(off High St.)
Old Acre GU21: Wok 5E 6
Oldacre GU24: W End 3F 3
Old Av. KT14: W Byf 4C 6
Old Av. Cl. KT14: W Byf 4C 6
Old Bakery Cl. GU6: Ewh 3K 37
Old Bakery M. GU5: Alb 2F 31
Old Barn Vw. GU7: G'mng 5J 33
Old Chertsey Rd. GU24: Chob 1D 4
Old Corn M. GU7: G'mng 1B 34
Old Ct. Rd. GU2: Guild 5C 22
Old Elstead Rd. GU8: Mil 5E 32
Old Epsom Rd. GU4: E Clan 1H 25
Old Farm Rd. GU1: Guild 1F 23
Oldfield Wood GU22: Wok 1K 11
Old Forge Ct. GU4: Shalf 3H 29
Old Grinstead GU5: Bram 1H 35
Old Hill GU22: Wok 4F 11
Oldhouse La. GU20: W'sham 1C 2
(not continuous)
Old Lodge Cl. GU7: G'mng 4H 33

Old Malt Way. GU21: Wok 1F 11
Old Mnr. Gdns. GU4: Guild 3A 30
Old Mnr. La. GU4: Guild 3A 30
Old Merrow St. GU4: Guild 1B 24
Old Oak Gdns. GU21: Wok 6F 5
Old Orchard KT14: Byfl 3K 7
Old Palace Rd. GU2: Guild 5C 22
Old Parvis Rd. KT14: W Byf 3G 7
Old Portsmouth Rd.
    GU3: Art, Peasm 6D 28
    GU3: Art, G'mng, Peasm 6D 28
Old Rectory Cl. GU5: Bram 1H 35
Old Rectory Gdns. GU7: Bus . . .5B 34
Old School Cl.
    GU1: Guild 2C 38 (4F 23)
Old School Pl. GU22: Wok 5G 11
Old Station Way GU7: G'mng . . .2A 34
OLD WOKING 5K 11
Old Woking Rd.
    GU22: Wok, Pyr 3A 12
    KT14: W Byf 4D 6
Omega Rd. GU21: Wok 7J 5
One Tree Hill Rd. GU4: Guild . . .5K 23
Onslow Cl. GU22: Wok 1J 11
Onslow Cres. GU22: Wok 1J 11
Onslow M. GU6: Cranl 5C 36
    (off High St.)
Onslow (Park & Ride) 6A 22
Onslow Rd. GU1: Guild . . .2D 38 (4F 23)
Onslow St. GU1: Guild 4B 38 (5E 22)
ONSLOW VILLAGE 6B 22
Onslow Way GU22: Pyr 6D 6
Opus Pk. GU1: Guild 7F 17
Orchard, The GU18: Light 2A 2
    GU21: Wok 7D 4
    GU22: Wok 6G 11
Orchard Av. KT15: Wdhm 2D 6
Orchard Cl. GU4: Guild 4K 23
    GU3: Flex 4B 20
    GU22: Wok 7K 5
    GU24: W End 4D 2
Orchard Cotts. GU4: Guild 3C 30
Orchard Dene KT14: W Byf 4E 6
    (off Madeira Rd.)
Orchard Dr. GU21: Wok 6G 5
Orchardfield Rd. GU7: G'mng . . .7B 28
Orchard Gdns. GU6: Cranl 6E 36
Orchard Ho. GU4: Guild 3B 24
    (off Merrow St.)
Orchard Lea Cl. GU22: Pyr 6C 6
Orchard Mains GU22: Wok 3E 10
Orchard M. GU21: Knap 2H 9
Orchard Rd. GU2: Guild 6B 22
    GU4: Burp 7K 17
    GU4: Shalf 3G 29
Orchards Cl. KT14: W Byf 5E 6
Orchard Way GU3: Flex 4B 20
    GU3: Worp 1K 15
    GU23: Send 2A 18
Orchid Dr. GU24: Bisl 6G 3
Oregano La. GU7: G'mng 7J 33
Oregano Way GU2: Guild 6C 16
Oriental Cl. GU22: Wok 1H 11
Oriental Rd. GU22: Wok 1H 11
Ormonde Rd. GU7: G'mng 1A 34
    GU21: Wok 7E 4
Osborne Dr. GU18: Light 2A 2
Oval, The GU2: Guild 5C 22
    GU3: Woo V 3H 21
    GU7: G'mng 7B 28
Overbrook GU7: G'mng 2C 34
Overford Cl. GU6: Cranl 6C 36
Overford Dr. GU6: Cranl 6D 36
Overthorpe Cl. GU21: Knap 1A 10
Ovington Ct. GU21: Wok 7B 4
Owen Rd. GU7: G'mng 1B 34
Oxford Rd. GU1: Guild . . .5D 38 (6F 23)
Oxford Ter. GU1: Guild . . .5D 38 (6F 23)
Oyster La. KT14: Byfl 1H 7

P

Paddock, The GU1: Guild 3B 24
    GU6: Cranl 5C 36
    GU6: Ewh 4K 37
    GU7: G'mng 4A 34
    GU18: Light 2A 2
Paddock Ho. GU4: Guild 3B 24
    (off Merrow St.)
Paddocks, The GU3: Flex 4C 20
    KT15: New H 1F 7
Paddocks Rd. GU4: Burp 7J 17
Paddock Way GU21: Wok 5K 5
Pageites GU7: G'mng 7H 27
Palace Ct. GU21: Wok 7J 5
    (off Maybury Rd.)
Palace Way GU22: Wok 4K 11
Palmers Lodge GU2: Guild 5C 22

Palmerston Cl. GU21: Wok 5J 5
Palm Gro. GU1: Guild 6E 16
Pannells Ct. GU1: Guild . . .4D 38 (5F 23)
Pantiles Ct. GU21: Wok 2D 10
Papercourt La. GU23: Rip 6D 12
Papercourt Sailing Club 6D 12
Parade, The GU2: Guild 6D 16
    (off Burden Way)
Paragon Cotts. GU4: E Clan 1H 25
Pares Cl. GU21: Wok 7F 5
Park & Ride
    Artington 2E 28
    Merrow 2E 28
    Onslow 6A 22
    Spectrum 2H 23
Park Av. GU8: P Har 2C 32
PARK BARN 3A 22
Park Barn Dr. GU2: Guild 2A 22
Park Barn E. GU2: Guild 3B 22
Park Barn Pde. GU2: Guild 4A 22
    (off Southway)
Park Chase GU1: Guild . . .2E 38 (4G 23)
    GU7: G'mng 5A 34
Park Cl. KT14: Byfl 4H 7
    KT15: New H 1F 7
Phillips Cl. GU7: G'mng 5K 33
Phillips Hatch GU5: Wone 6A 30
Phillip's Quad. GU2: Wok 2G 11
Philpot La. GU24: Chob 4D 4
Phoenix Ct. GU1: Guild . . .5C 38 (6F 23)
Piccards, The GU2: Guild 1E 28
Pickering Pl. GU2: Guild 2C 22
Pilgrim Ct. GU8: Mil 7F 33
Pilgrim's Cl. GU5: Shere 2K 31
Pilgrim's Way GU5: Shere 2K 31
    GU24: Bisl 7G 3
Pilgrims' Way GU4: Guild 1F 29
    GU5: Alb 7D 24
Pimms Cl. GU4: Burp 7J 17
Pine Cl. GU21: Wok 7E 4
    KT15: New H 2F 7
Pinehurst GU22: Wok 2F 11
    (off Park Dr.)
Pine Pk. GU3: Worp 6G 15
Pine Rd. GU22: Wok 4E 10
Pines, The GU21: Wok 5H 5
Pines Trad. Est., The
    GU3: Guild 2A 22
Pine Tree Hill GU22: Pyr 7B 6
Pine Vw. Cl. GU4: Guild 3D 30
Pinewood Av. KT15: New H 1G 7
Pinewood Cl. GU21: Wok 1G 7
Pinewood Dr. KT15: New H 1G 7
Pinewood Gro. KT15: New H 1F 7
Pinewood Pk. KT15: New H 2F 7
PINKS HILL 2J 21
Pinks M. GU8: Mil 7F 33
PIRBRIGHT 7F 9
PIRBRIGHT CAMP 7F 9
Pirbright Golf Course 5D 8
Pirbright Grn. GU24: Pirb 7F 9
Pirbright Rd. GU3: Norm 1A 20
Pirbright Ter. GU24: Pirb 7F 9
PITCH PLACE 6C 16
Pit Farm Rd. GU1: Guild 4J 23
Pit Farm Tennis Club 4J 23
Pitt Rivers Cl. GU1: Guild 5K 23
Platt M. GU4: Guild 1B 24
Plough La. GU6: Ewh 4K 37
Plovers Ri. GU24: Brkwd 4E 8
Point, The GU21: Wok 7H 5
    (off Chertsey Rd.)
Polesden La. GU23: Rip 7D 12
Pollard Rd. GU22: Wok 7K 5
Polsted La. GU3: Comp 4H 27
Poltimore Rd. GU2: Guild 6C 22
Pondfield Rd. GU7: G'mng 7B 28
Pond Mdw. GU2: Guild 4A 22
Pond Rd. GU24: Bisl 4C 10
Ponds La. GU5: Alb 5J 31
Poole Rd. GU21: Wok 2G 11
Pool in the Pk. 3H 11
Poplar Cotts. GU3: Guild 1A 22
Poplar Gro. GU22: Wok 3G 11
Poplar Rd. GU4: Shalf 4G 29
Porridge Pot All.
    GU1: Guild 6B 38 (6F 23)
Portland Ter. GU1: Guild 5G 23
    (off Harvey Rd.)
Portsmouth Rd.
    GU2: Guild 7B 38 (1E 28)
    GU3: Art 1E 28
    GU7: G'mng 6G 33
    GU8: G'mng, Mil 6G 33
    GU8: Mil, Thur 7C 32
    GU23: Rip, Wis 5H 13
    GU3: Send, Rip 2D 18
Portugal Rd. GU21: Wok 7H 5
Port Way GU24: Bisl 7G 3
Postford Farm Cotts. GU5: Alb . . .4E 30

Peper Harow La. GU8: Shack 1C 32
Peper Harow Pk. GU8: P Har 2C 32
Peperharow Rd. GU7: G'mng . . .1H 33
Percheron Dr. GU21: Knap 3J 9
Percy Rd. GU2: Guild 2D 22
Peregrine Cl. GU6: Cranl 4D 36
Perleybrooke La. GU21: Wok 1C 10
Perrin Ct. GU21: Wok 6K 5
Perrior Rd. GU7: G'mng 7A 28
Perry Cl. GU7: G'mng 2C 34
Perry Hill GU3: Worp 4A 16
    (not continuous)
Perseverance Cotts. GU23: Rip . .5G 13
Petersham Av. KT14: Byfl 3J 7
Petersham Cl. KT14: Byfl 3J 7
Petworth Rd. GU8: Mil 7E 32
Pewley Bank GU1: Guild 6G 23
Pewley Down (Local Nature Reserve)
    . . . . .7H 23
Pewley Hill GU1: Guild . . .5D 38 (6F 23)
Pewley Point GU1: Guild 6G 23
Pewley Way GU1: Guild 6G 23
Pheasant Cl. GU8: Mil 7F 33

Peper Harow La. GU8: Shack 1C 32
Postford Mill Cotts. GU4: Guild . . .1D 30
Potters Cl. GU8: Mil 5F 33
Potters La. GU23: Send 7K 11
Pound Cl. GU7: G'mng 3A 34
Pound Ct. GU3: Woo V 3H 21
Pound Fld. GU1: Guild 1C 38 (3F 23)
Poundfield Ct. GU22: Wok 5A 12
Poundfield Gdns. GU22: Wok 4A 12
    (not continuous)
Pound Hill GU3: Woo V 3H 21
Pound La. GU3: Woo V 3H 21
    GU7: G'mng 3A 34
    (not continuous)
Pound La. Cvn. Site
    GU3: Woo V 3H 21
Pound Pl. GU4: Shalf 3H 29
Pound Pl. Cl. GU4: Shalf 3H 29
Powderham Ct. GU21: Knap 2K 9
Powell Cl. GU2: Guild 6B 22
Power Cl. GU1: Guild 1B 38 (3E 22)
Poyle Ho. GU4: Guild 3B 24
    (off Merrow St.)
Poyle Rd. GU1: Guild 6G 23
Poyle Ter. GU1: Guild 5D 38 (6F 23)
Precinct, The GU6: Cranl 4D 36
Presbury Ct. GU21: Wok 2C 10
PREY HEATH 7E 10
Prey Heath Cl. GU22: Wok 1E 16
Prey Heath Rd. GU22: Wok 1D 16
Priest La. GU24: W End 4C 2
Priestley Rd. GU2: Guild 4K 21
Priestly Gdns. GU22: Wok 4J 11
Prime Pl. Row GU7: G'mng 3A 34
    (off Catteshall La.)
Primrose Dr. GU24: Bisl 6G 3
Primrose Pl. GU7: G'mng 5H 33
Primrose Ridge GU7: G'mng 5H 33
Primrose Way GU5: Bram 2F 35
Prince's Av. GU7: G'mng 7J 27
Princes Ct. GU1: Guild 1C 38
Princess Gdns. GU22: Wok 7K 5
Princess Mary Cl. GU2: Guild . . .7C 16
Princess Rd. GU22: Wok 7K 5
Printing Ho. Sq.
    GU1: Guild 4C 38 (5F 23)
Priors Ct. GU21: Wok 2C 10
Prior's Cft. GU22: Wok 4J 11
Priorsfield Rd. GU3: Comp 3F 27
    GU7: Hurt 3F 27
Priors Hatch La. GU7: Hurt 5F 27
Priorswood GU3: Comp 4F 27
Priory Cl. GU1: Guild 4B 6
Priory Ct. GU2: Guild 1E 28
Providence Pl. GU22: Pyr 5E 6
Prunus Cl. GU24: W End 4E 2
Pucks Hill GU21: Knap 1K 9
Pullman La. GU7: G'mng 5J 33
Purbeck Ct. GU2: Guild 4A 22
Purbeck Dr. GU21: Wok 5H 5
PUTTENHAM 2C 26
Puttenham Golf Course 2D 26
Puttenham Heath Rd.
    GU3: Comp, Putt 2D 26
Puttenham Hill GU3: Putt 1C 26
Puttenham La. GU8: Shack 5C 26
PYLE HILL 1F 17
Pyle Hill GU22: Wok 1F 17
PYRFORD 7E 6
Pyrford Comn. Rd. GU22: Pyr . . .7B 6
Pyrford Ct. GU22: Pyr 1C 12
Pyrford Golf Course 1F 13
PYRFORD GREEN 1F 13
Pyrford Heath GU22: Pyr 7D 6
Pyrford Lock GU23: Wis 7G 7
Pyrford Rd. GU22: Pyr 4E 6
    KT14: W Byf 4E 6
PYRFORD VILLAGE 2E 12
Pyrford Wood Est. GU22: Pyr 7D 6
Pyrford Woods Cl. GU22: Pyr 6C 6
Pyrford Woods Cl. GU22: Pyr 6D 6
Pyrian Cl. GU22: Wok 7B 6

Q

Quadrangle, The GU2: Guild 5C 22
Quadrant, The GU1: Guild 4B 38
    (off Bridge St.)
Quadrum Pk. GU3: Peasm 4D 28
Quakers Way GU3: Worp 7J 15
Quarry Bank GU18: Light 2A 2
Quarry Hill GU7: G'mng 4H 33
Quarry Rd. GU7: Hurt 7G 27
Quarry St. GU1: Guild 5C 38 (6F 23)
Quartermaine Av. GU22: Wok . . .6H 11
Quartermile Rd. GU7: G'mng 5A 34
Queendale Ct. GU21: Wok 7B 4
Queen Eleanor's Rd.
    GU2: Guild 5B 22
QUEEN ELIZABETH PARK 7C 16

Palmers Lodge GU2: Guild 5C 22
Park Dr. GU5: Bram 1H 35
    GU6: Cranl 4E 36
    GU22: Wok 2H 11
Parkfield GU7: Bus 5A 34
Park Ga. Cotts. GU6: Cranl 5A 36
Park Ga. Ct. GU22: Wok 2G 11
Park Hgts. GU22: Guild 2G 11
    (off Constitution Hill)
Parkhurst Rd. GU2: Guild 3C 22
PARKLANDS 4K 31
Parklands GU2: Guild 7C 16
Parklands Cotts. GU5: Shere 4K 31
Parklands Dr. GU6: Cranl 5F 37
Parklands Pl. GU1: Guild 2H 11
Park La. GU4: Guild 1B 24
Parkmead GU6: Cranl 4E 36
Park Pl. GU22: Wok 2H 11
    (off Hill Vw. Rd.)
Park Rd. GU1: Guild 2C 38 (4F 23)
    GU5: Guild 3J 31
    GU7: G'mng 5A 34
    GU21: Wok 1H 11
    (not continuous)
Parkside KT15: New H 2F 7
Parkside Cotts. GU4: W Cla 2E 24
Park St. GU1: Guild 5B 38 (6E 22)
Park Vw. Ct. GU22: Guild 3H 11
Parkview La. GU4: Guild 3H 7
Parkway GU1: Guild 3G 23
Parley Dr. GU21: Wok 1E 10
Parliamentary Rd. GU24: Brkwd . .5A 8
Parnham Av. GU18: Light 2D 2
Parr Ct. GU21: Knap 3J 9
    (off Tudor Way)
Parry Dr. KT13: Weybr 1K 7
Parsonage Rd. GU6: Cranl 5C 36
Parsons Grn. GU1: Guild 2F 23
Parsons Grn. Ct. GU1: Guild 1F 23
Partridge Way GU4: Guild 2B 24
Parvis Rd. KT14: W Byf, Byfl 4F 7
Pathfields GU5: Shere 3K 31
Pathway, The GU23: Send 2D 18
Pavilion Ct. GU6: Cranl 5B 36
    (off East Vw. La.)
Pavilions, The KT14: Byfl 2H 7
Paxton Gdns. GU21: Wok 3B 6
Paynter Ct. GU1: Guild 1E 22
Peacocks Shop. Cen., The
    GU21: Wok 1G 11
Peak Fitness
    Woking 1H 11
    (off Chertsey Rd.)
Peak Rd. GU2: Guild 1C 22
Pearl Ct. GU21: Wok 7A 4
Peamore Av. GU22: Pyr 7E 6
Peatmore Cl. GU22: Pyr 7E 6
Peatmore Dr. GU24: Brkwd 5C 8
Pembroke Gdns. GU22: Wok 2J 11
Pembroke Rd. GU22: Wok 2J 11
Pendennis Cl. KT14: W Byf 5E 6
Pengilly Ho. GU1: Guild 4A 24
Penhurst GU21: Wok 5H 5
Pennings Av. GU2: Guild 2B 22
Penny Dr. GU3: Woo V 3H 21
PENNY POT 3J 3
Pennypot La. GU24: Chob 4H 3
Penstock M. GU7: G'mng 2C 34
Pentire Cl. GU21: Wok 5G 5
Pentreath Av. GU2: Guild 5B 22
Penwith Wlk. GU22: Wok 3J 11
Penwood End GU22: Wok 5D 10
PEPER HAROW 2C 32

Queen Elizabeth Way
  GU22: Wok 3H 11
Queenhythe Cres. GU4: Jac W . . .5F 17
Queenhythe Rd. GU4: Jac W . . .5F 17
Queen Mary Cl. GU22: Wok 7A 6
Queen Mary's Dr. KT15: New H . . .1D 6
Queen's Av. GU14: Byfl 3H 7
Queens Cl. GU24: Bisl 7G 3
Queens Ct. GU1: Guild 2D 38
  GU22: Wok 2H 11
Queen's Dr. GU7: G'mng 7H 27
Queens Dr. GU2: Guild 1C 22
Queens Ga. GU7: G'mng 3A 34
  (off Queen St.)
Queen's Rd. GU1: Guild . . .2D 38 (4F 23)
  GU21: Knap 2J 9
Queens Rd. GU24: Bisl, Brkwd 4E 8
Queen St. GU7: G'mng 3A 34
Queen's Way GU24: Brkwd 3D 8
Queensway GU6: Cranl 6E 36
Queenswood Rd. GU21: Wok 3K 9
Queen Victoria Rd.
  GU24: Brkwd 3D 8
Quiet Cnr. GU7: G'mng 1A 34
Quince Dr. GU24: Bisl 6H 3
Quintrell Cl. GU21: Wok 1D 10

R

Rack's Ct. GU1: Guild 6D 38 (6F 23)
Racquets Ct. Hill GU7: G'mng . .1J 33
Radstone Cl. GU22: Wok 2H 11
Raeburn Ct. GU2: Wok 3C 10
Raeburn Gro. GU21: Wok 2C 10
Rafdene Copse GU22: Wok 3E 10
Raglan Rd. GU21: Knap, Wok . . .2A 10
Rails La. GU24: Pirb 2C 14
Railton Rd. GU2: Guild 7D 16
Rainbow Ct. GU21: Wok 7A 4
Rake La. GU8: Mil 7G 33
Ramin Ct. GU1: Guild 1E 22
Ramsden Rd. GU7: G'mng 4K 33
Randolph Cl. GU21: Knap 1A 10
Range, The GU5: Bram 3J 35
Rapley's Fld. GU24: Pirb 7E 8
Rapsley La. GU21: Knap 2H 9
Ravens Cl. GU21: Wok 7J 3
Ravenswood Ct. GU22: Wok 2H 11
Raymond Cres. GU2: Guild 5B 22
Raynes Cl. GU21: Wok 1A 10
Raynham Cl. GU4: Burp 7K 17
Recreation Rd.
  GU1: Guild 1B 38 (4F 23)
Rectory Cl. GU4: Guild 2B 24
  GU6: Ewh 3K 37
  GU7: Bus 5B 34
  KT14: Byfl 4H 7
Rectory Gdn. GU6: Cranl 5C 36
Rectory La. GU5: Shere 2K 31
  KT14: Byfl 4J 7
Redcourt GU22: Pyr 6B 6
Redcroft Wlk. GU6: Cranl 6D 36
Redding Way GU21: Knap 3H 9
Red Rd. GU18: Light 3A 2
Redwing Av. GU7: G'mng 5K 27
Redwing Gdns. KT14: W Byf 3F 7
Redwing Ri. GU4: Guild 2B 24
Redwood Gro. GU4: Guild 3A 30
Reed Pl. KT14: W Byf 4C 6
Reeve Ct. GU2: Guild 7C 16
  (off Tarragon Rd.)
Regal Ct. GU1: Guild 1D 38
Regalfield Cl. GU2: Guild 7B 16
Regan Cl. GU2: Guild 6D 16
Regency Dr. KT14: W Byf 4D 6
Regent Cl. KT15: New H 1H 7
Regent Ct. GU2: Guild 2D 22
REIDON HILL 2H 9
Reidonhill Cotts. GU21: Knap 2H 9
Reindorp Cl. GU2: Guild 5C 22
Reris Grange Cl. GU8: Mil 5F 33
Restwell Av. GU6: Cranl 2A 36
Retreat, The GU6: Cranl 4B 36
Revesby Cl. GU24: W End 4D 2
Rhoda McGaw Theatre 1G 11
RHS Garden Wisley 2J 13
Ricardo Ct. GU5: Bram 6H 11
Rices Cnr. GU4: Shalf 5J 29
Richard Meyjes Rd. GU2: Guild . .5A 22
Richmond Rd. GU7: G'mng 1K 33
Rickford GU3: Worp 3K 15
Rickford Hill GU3: Worp 3K 15
Rickyard GU2: Guild 4K 21
Ride La. GU5: Alb 7H 31
Ridge, The GU24: Wok 1K 11
Ridge Cl. GU22: Wok 5D 10
Ridgemount GU2: Guild 5D 22
Ridges, The GU3: Art 2E 28
Ridgeway GU21: Wok 6F 5

Ridgeway, The GU1: Guild 5J 23
  GU6: Cranl 5E 36
  GU18: Light 1B 2
  GU24: Brkwd 4F 9
Ridgeway Cl. GU6: Cranl 5F 37
  GU18: Light 2A 2
  GU21: Wok 6F 5
Ridgeway Gdns. GU21: Wok 6F 5
RIDGWAY 6E 6
Ridgway Rd. GU2: Pyr 6E 6
Ridgway Rd. GU2: Pyr 6D 6
Riding, The GU21: Wok 5K 5
Ridings, The GU6: Cranl 4D 36
  GU23: Rip 7E 12
Ridsdale Rd. GU21: Wok 1D 10
Ringmore Dr. GU4: Guild 1A 24
RIPLEY .5G 13
Ripley By-Pass GU23: Rip 7G 13
Ripley La. GU23: Rip 7J 13
Ripley Rd. GU4: E Clan 6H 19
Ripon Cl. GU2: Guild 2B 22
River Cl. GU1: Guild 2E 22
River Ct. GU21: Wok 5A 6
Riverdale Dr. GU22: Wok 5H 11
Rivermead KT14: Byfl 4K 7
Rivermead Wlk. GU21: Wok 2B 34
Rivermount Gdns. GU2: Guild 7E 22
Riverside GU2: Guild 2F 23
Riverside Av. GU18: Light 2C 2
Riverside Bus. Cen.
  GU1: Guild 2A 38 (4E 22)
Riverside Cl. GU21: Wok 4F 9
Riverside Cl. GU5: Bram 7J 29
Riverside Ct. GU22: Wok 5K 11
Riverside Pk. (Local Nature Reserve)
  . . . . .1G 23
Riverside Wlk. GU7: G'mng 2K 33
Riverview GU1: Guild . . .1A 38 (4E 22)
Riverway Est. GU3: Peasm 6E 28
Riverwood Cl. GU2: Guild 2E 22
Rivett Drake Cl. GU2: Guild 7D 16
Rivey Cl. KT14: W Byf 5D 6
Road Ho. Est. GU22: Wok 5J 11
Robertson Ct. GU21: Wok 2A 10
Roberts Way GU6: Cranl 4D 36
Robin Hill GU7: G'mng 7K 27
Robin Hood Cl. GU21: Wok 2B 10
Robin Hood Cres. GU21: Knap . . .1A 10
Robin Hood La. GU4: Sut G 1H 17
Robin Hood Rd.
  GU21: Knap, Wok 1K 9
  (not continuous)
Robin Hood Works GU21: Knap . . .1K 9
Robinettes Ct. GU7: G'mng 7H 27
Robins Dale GU21: Knap 1J 9
Robinson Ct. GU2: Guild 4A 12
Robin Way GU2: Guild 7D 16
Rodborough Common (Nature Reserve)
  . . . . .7C 32
Rodborough Hill Cotts.
  GU8: Mil 7C 32
Rodney Way GU1: Guild 3J 23
Rodsall La. GU3: Putt 6A 26
Roffords GU21: Wok 1B 10
Rokeby Ct. GU21: Wok 1B 10
Roker Pk. Golf Course 6K 15
Rokers La. GU8: Shack 7D 26
Roman Farm Rd. GU2: Guild 3K 21
Romans Cl. GU1: Guild 5K 23
Romans Way GU22: Pyr 6E 6
Romany Rd. GU21: Knap 6J 3
Ronald Ross Rd. GU2: Guild 5A 22
Rooks Hill GU5: Bram 5K 35
Rookwood Ct.
  GU2: Guild 7A 38 (7E 22)
Rosalind Franklin Cl.
  GU2: Guild 5A 22
Roseacre Gdns. GU4: Guild 3D 30
Rose Bank Cotts. GU6: Cranl 6G 11
Rosebery Cres. GU22: Wok 4H 11
Rosebriar Cl. GU22: Pyr 7E 6
Rosebury Dr. GU24: Bisl 6G 3
Rosehill Av. GU21: Wok 7E 4
Rose La. GU23: Rip 5G 13
Rosemary Cres. GU2: Guild 7B 16
Rosemary Gdns. GU7: G'mng 7J 33
Rose Mdw. GU24: W End 4G 3
Rosemount Av. KT14: W Byf 4E 6
Rosemount Point KT14: W Byf 4E 6
  (off Rosemount Av.)
Rose Pk. KT15: Wdhm 1C 6
Rosetrees GU1: Guild 5J 23
Rosewarne Cl. GU21: Wok 2C 10
Rosewood GU22: Wok 3J 11
Rosewood Ct. KT14: Byfl 3J 7
Rosewood Way GU24: W End 4E 2
Roslyn Ct. GU21: Wok 2B 10
Rossiter Lodge GU1: Guild 5J 23
Rough, The GU22: Wok 1B 10

Roughlands GU22: Pyr 6C 6
Rough Rd. GU22: Wok 6J 9
Rounce La. GU24: W End 4D 2
Roundhill GU22: Wok 3K 11
Roundhill Dr. GU22: Wok 2K 11
Roundhill Way GU2: Guild 4B 22
Roundthorn Way GU21: Wok 7B 4
Rowan Cl. GU1: Guild 1D 22
Rowan Dr. GU7: G'mng 7J 33
Rowans, The GU22: Wok 2G 11
Rowbury GU7: G'mng 6C 28
Rowe La. GU24: Pirb 1G 15
Rowland Rd. GU6: Cranl 5C 36
Row La. GU5: Alb 7J 31
ROWLEY 2A 36
Rowley Cl. GU22: Pyr 7F 7
Rowly Dr. GU6: Cranl 2B 36
Rowly Edge GU6: Cranl 2A 36
Royal Horticultural Society Cotts.
  GU23: Wis 7J 7
Royal Oak Rd. GU21: Wok 2E 10
Royals, The GU1: Guild 4D 38
ROYAL SURREY COUNTY HOSPITAL
  . . . . .4A 22
Royston Av. KT14: Byfl 3J 7
Royston Pk. KT14: Byfl 3J 7
Royston Rd. KT14: Byfl 3J 7
Rubus Cl. GU24: W End 4E 2
Rubus Cl. GU24: W End 4E 2
Rugosa Rd. GU24: W End 4E 2
Runtley Wood La.
  GU4: Sut G 2H 17
Rupert Rd. GU2: Guild 4A 38 (5E 22)
Ruscoe Dr. GU22: Wok 2J 11
Rush Ct. GU7: G'mng 6C 28
RUSHETT COMMON 6K 35
Rushmoor Cl. GU2: Guild 1B 22
Russell Cl. GU21: Wok 6E 4
Russell Ct. GU1: Guild 1E 22
Russell Rd. GU21: Wok 6E 4
Russetts Cl. GU21: Wok 6H 5
Rutson Rd. KT14: Byfl 5K 7
Ruxley Cl. GU22: Wok 3F 11
  (off West Hill Rd.)
Rydal Pl. GU18: Light 2B 2
Ryde Cl. GU23: Rip 5G 13
Ryde Heron GU21: Knap 1A 10
Ryde Lands GU6: Cranl 4E 36
Rydens Pde. GU22: Wok 4K 11
Rydens Way GU22: Wok 4J 11
Rydes Av. GU2: Guild 1B 22
Rydes Cl. GU22: Wok 4A 12
RYDESHILL 2A 22
Ryde's Hill Cres. GU2: Guild 7B 16
Ryde's Hill Rd. GU2: Guild 1A 22
Rye Cl. GU2: Guild 2A 22
Rye Gro. GU6: Cranl 5A 36
  GU18: Light 1F 3

S

Sadlers Cl. GU4: Guild 3B 24
Saffron Platt GU2: Guild 7C 16
St Albans Cl. GU3: Woo V 3H 21
St Andrews GU6: Cranl 4A 36
St Andrews Cl. GU21: Wok 1E 10
St Andrew's Ga. GU22: Wok 2H 11
St Anne's Rd. GU7: G'mng 2C 34
St Anns GU22: Wok 2G 11
St Bartholomews Ct.
  GU1: Guild 6H 23
St Catherines GU2: Guild 3E 10
St Catherine's Ct. GU5: Bram 7H 29
St Catherine's Dr. GU2: Guild 1D 28
St Catherine's Hill GU2: Guild 1E 28
St Catherines Pk.
  GU1: Guild 6H 23
St Denys Cl. GU21: Knap 2K 9
St Edmund's Steps GU7: G'mng . .3K 33
St Fillans GU21: Wok 1K 9
St Hilda's Cl. GU21: Knap 1K 9
St James Cl. GU21: Wok 2C 10
St James's Pl. GU6: Cranl 5B 36
ST JOHNS 2C 10
St John's Cl. GU2: Guild 5C 22
St John's Ct. GU24: Brkwd 4F 9
St Johns Ct. GU21: Wok 3C 10
St John's Gdns. GU21: Wok 2C 10
  (off St John's Rd.)
St John's Hill Rd. GU21: Wok 3C 10
St Johns Lodge GU21: Wok 3C 10
St John's Lye GU21: Wok 3A 10
St John's M. GU21: Wok 2C 10
St John's Ri. GU21: Wok 3D 10
St John's Rd. GU2: Guild 5B 22
  GU21: Wok 3C 10
St John's St. GU7: G'mng 1B 34
St Johns Waterside GU21: Wok . . .2C 10
  (off Copse Rd.)
St Lawrence Ct. GU24: Chob 2A 4

St Lawrence Ho. GU24: Chob 2A 4
  (off Bagshot Rd.)
St Lukes Ct. GU21: Wok 5A 6
St Lukes Sq. GU1: Guild 5H 23
St Margaret's GU1: Guild 4H 23
St Mark's Ct. GU22: Wok 3G 11
  (off Brooklyn Rd.)
St Martha's Av. GU22: Wok 5H 11
St Marthas Ct. GU4: Guild 3K 29
St Martins M. GU22: Pyr 7E 6
St Marys Gdn. GU3: Worp 4A 16
St Mary's Rd. GU21: Wok 1E 10
St Mary's Ter. GU1: Guild 5C 38
St Marys Way GU2: Guild 2A 22
St Michael's Av. GU3: Worp 6J 15
St Michael's Rd. GU21: Wok 5B 6
St Mildred's Rd. GU1: Guild 3H 23
St Nicholas Cres. GU22: Pyr 7E 6
St Nicolas Av. GU6: Cranl 5D 36
St Nicolas Ct. GU6: Cranl 5D 36
St Omer Ridge GU1: Guild 5J 23
St Omer Rd. GU1: Guild 5J 23
St Paul's Rd. GU22: Wok 1J 11
St Peter's Cl. GU22: Wok 4A 12
St Peter's Rd. GU22: Wok 5H 11
St Saviours Pl.
  GU1: Guild 2B 38 (4E 22)
St Thomas Cl. GU4: Guild 3A 30
  GU21: Wok 1E 10
St Thomas Dr. GU4: E Clan 1J 25
St Thomas's M. GU1: Guild 6H 23
Salisbury Pit. KT14: W Byf 2G 7
Salisbury Rd. GU22: Wok 3G 11
Salt Box Cotts. GU2: Guild 6C 16
Salt Box Rd. GU3: Guild 6B 16
  GU4: Guild 6B 16
Salvia Cl. GU24: Bisl 7G 3
Sample Oak La.
  GU4: Blckh, Guild 3C 30
Sandalwood GU22: Wok 5D 22
Sandfield Ct. GU1: Guild 3C 38
Sandfields GU21: Send 1B 18
Sandfield Ter.
  GU1: Guild 3C 38 (5F 23)
Sandpit Cotts. GU24: Pirb 6E 8
Sandpit Hall Rd. GU24: Chob 3C 4
Sandpit Heath GU3: Worp 7K 15
Sandpit La. GU21: Knap 5H 3
  (not continuous)
Sandringham Cl. GU22: Pyr 7E 6
Sandy Cl. GU22: Wok 1A 12
Sandy La. GU3: Art 2C 28
  GU3: Art, Comp 2K 27
  GU3: Norm, Woo V 1E 20
  GU5: Alb 4G 31
  GU7: G'mng 1K 33
  GU8: Mil 7E 32
  GU22: Pyr 1E 12
  (not continuous)
  GU22: Wok 1K 11
  GU23: Send 7A 12
Sandy Way GU22: Wok 1A 12
Sanger Dr. GU23: Send 7A 12
SANWAY .5J 7
Sanway Cl. KT14: Byfl 5J 7
Sanway Rd. KT14: Byfl 5J 7
Sapley Cl. GU21: Wok 7A 4
Sapte Cl. GU6: Cranl 5F 37
Sarus Pl. GU6: Cranl 5C 36
Saunderites GU7: G'mng 7J 27
Saunders Copse GU22: Wok 6D 10
Saunders La. GU22: Wok 6A 10
Sawpit La. GU4: E Clan 1J 25
Saxon Cl. GU7: G'mng 2B 34
Saxon Way GU1: Guild 5K 23
Sayers Croft Local Nature Reserve
  . . . . .3H 37
Scarlett Cl. GU21: Wok 2B 10
Scholars Wlk. GU2: Guild 5D 22
School Cl. GU1: Guild 1F 23
  GU24: Bisl 6F 3
School Cotts. GU22: Wok 6E 10
  (off Mayford Grn.)
School La. GU3: Norm 1A 20
  GU3: Putt 2C 26
  GU4: E Clan 1J 25
  GU8: Shack 1E 32
  GU24: Pirb 6E 8
School Mdw. GU22: Guild 2K 21
Scillonian Rd. GU2: Guild 5C 22
Scizdons Climb GU7: G'mng 3B 34
Scotland Bri. Lock
  KT15: New H 2E 6
Scotland Bri. Rd. KT15: New H . . .2E 6
Scotswood Pk. GU21: Wok 5B 6
Scott Cl. GU2: Guild 2C 22
Scott's Gro. Cl. GU24: Chob 4K 3
Scott's Gro. Rd. GU24: Chob 4H 3
Scutley La. GU18: Light 1E 2
Scylla Pl. GU21: Wok 3C 10

Seale La. GU3: Putt 2A 26
  GU10: Seale 2A 26
Searlwood Cl. GU24: W End 5F 3
Sefton Cl. GU24: W End 4F 3
Selbourne Rd. KT15: New H 1F 7
Selbourne Cl. KT15: New H 1F 7
Selbourne Rd. GU4: Burp 1J 23
Selby Wlk. GU21: Wok 2D 10
Selhurst Cl. GU21: Wok 6H 5
Sellar's Hill GU7: G'mng 7K 27
Sells Cl. GU1: Guild 6H 23
Selsdon Rd. KT15: New H 2E 6
Seltops Cl. GU6: Cranl 6E 36
Selwood Rd. GU22: Wok 4K 11
Semaphore Rd.
  GU1: Guild 6E 38 (6G 23)
Semper Cl. GU21: Knap 1A 10
SEND .7B 12
Send & Ripley History Society Mus.
  . . . . .5F 13
Send Barns La. GU23: Send 1B 18
Send Cl. GU23: Send 7A 12
Send Hill GU23: Send 2A 18
SEND MARSH 7D 12
Send Marsh Grn. GU23: Rip 7D 12
Send Marsh Rd.
  GU23: Rip, Send 7A 12
Send Pde. Cl. GU23: Send 7A 12
Send Rd. GU23: Send 6K 11
Servite Ho. GU21: Knap 1K 9
Seymour Pl. GU22: Wok 4D 10
Seymour Rd. GU7: G'mng 4H 33
SHACKLEFORD 7D 26
Shackleford Grn. GU8: Shack 7D 26
Shackleford Rd.
  GU8: Els, Shack 3A 32
  GU8: Shack 7D 26
  GU22: Wok 4J 11
Shackleton Wlk. GU2: Guild 4B 22
  (off Humbolt Cl.)
Shackstead La. GU7: G'mng 4J 33
Shadyhanger GU7: G'mng 1A 34
Shaftesbury Rd. GU22: Wok 1K 11
  GU24: Bisl 7F 3
SHALFORD 3G 29
Shalford Mill 2G 29
Shalford Rd.
  GU1: Guild 7D 38 (7F 23)
  GU4: Guild 7F 23
Shalford Station (Rail) 3G 29
Shambles, The
  GU1: Guild 5C 38 (6F 23)
Shamrock Cotts. GU3: Worp 5D 16
Shaws Cotts. GU2: Guild 6B 16
  (off Weydown La.)
Sheepfold Rd. GU2: Guild 1B 22
Sheeplands Av. GU1: Guild 2A 24
Sheep Wlk., The GU22: Wok 2B 12
SHEERWATER 5B 6
Sheerwater Av. KT15: Wdhm 3C 6
Sheerwater Bus. Cen.
  GU21: Wok 6A 6
Sheerwater Rd. GU21: Wok 3C 6
  KT14: W Byf 3C 6
  KT15: Wdhm 3C 6
SHEET'S HEATH 3F 9
Sheet's Heath La. GU24: Brkwd . .3G 9
Sheldon Cl. GU1: Guild 5H 23
Shelton Cl. GU2: Guild 6C 16
Shepherd's Hill GU1: Guild 2C 22
Shepherd's La. GU2: Guild 1B 22
Shepherd's Way GU4: Guild 1G 29
Sherborne Ct.
  GU1: Guild 5B 38 (6E 22)
Sherborne Cl. GU5: Alb 2H 31
Sherborne Cotts. GU5: Alb 1J 31
Sherborne Farm 7J 25
SHERE 2K 31
Shere Rd. GU4: Guild, W Cla 5E 24
  GU5: Alb, Shere 1H 31
  GU6: Ewh 1J 37
Shere Woodlands Local Nature Reserve
  . . . . .7K 25
Sherrydon GU6: Cranl 4E 36
Sherwood Rd. GU21: Knap 1A 10
Shetland Cl. GU4: Burp 6K 17
Shey Copse GU22: Wok 1A 12
Shilburn Way GU21: Wok 2C 10
Shimmings, The GU1: Guild 3J 23
Shires Ho. KT14: Byfl 4J 7
Shirley Cl. GU1: Guild 3D 38
Shirley Pl. GU21: Wok 1A 10
Shophouse La. GU5: Alb 7H 31
Shops, The GU5: Wone 6K 29
Shores Rd. GU21: Wok 5G 5
Shortwood GU22: Wok 3F 11
  (off Mt. Hermon Rd.)
Shrubs Hill GU24: Chob 1J 3
Shrublands Dr. GU18: Light 2B 2
Sidney Ct. GU3: Guild 7A 16

Silent Pool 7H 25
Silistria Cl. GU21: Knap 2J 9
Silo Cl. GU7: G'mng 6B 28
Silo Dr. GU7: G'mng 6B 28
Silo Rd. GU7: G'mng 6B 28
Silver Birch Cl. KT15: Wdhm 3C 6
Silversmiths Way GU21: Wok 2E 10
Silverwood GU6: Cranl 2A 36
Silverwood Cotts. GU5: Alb 1J 31
Sime Cl. GU3: Guild 7B 16
Simmond's Cotts. GU7: G'mng . . .3H 33
Simmons Ct. GU1: Guild 7E 16
Slade Rd. GU4: Brkwd 4D 8
Slapleys GU22: Wok 4G 11
Slip of Wood GU6: Cranl 4D 36
Slocock Hill GU21: Wok 1E 10
Slyfield Cl. GU1: Guild 1G 23
Slyfield Grn. GU1: Guild 1F 23
SLYFIELD GREEN 1F 23
Slyfield Grn. GU1: Guild 7G 17
Slyfield Ind. Est. GU1: Guild 7G 17
Smart's Heath La. GU22: Wok 7C 10
Smart's Heath Rd. GU22: Wok . . .7B 10
Smeaton Dr. GU22: Wok 4K 11
Smiles Pl. GU22: Wok 7K 5
Smith Ct. GU21: Wok 4B 6
Smithwood Av. GU6: Cranl 1A 36
SMITHWOOD COMMON 1B 36
Smithwood Comn. Rd.
  GU6: Cranl 1A 36
Snelgate Cotts. GU4: E Clan 1H 25
Snowdenham La. GU5: Bram 3F 35
Snowdenham Links Rd.
  GU5: Bram 1F 35
Snowdrop Way GU24: Bisl 1G 9
Snoxhall Fld. GU6: Cranl 6C 36
Sol-y-Vista GU7: G'mng 1K 33
Somerset Ho. GU22: Wok 4C 10
  (off Oriental Rd.)
Somerswey GU4: Shalf 5G 29
Somertons Cl. GU2: Guild 1C 22
Sonic Ct. GU1: Guild 1B 38 (3E 22)
Sopwith Dr. KT13: Weyb 2J 7
Sorrel Dr. GU18: Light 3A 2
Southbury GU2: Guild 6B 38
South Cl. GU21: Wok 7E 4
Southcote GU21: Wok 6F 5
South Dr. GU24: Brkwd 5C 8
Southern Bungs. GU4: Guild 4K 29
South Farm La. GU18: Light 1A 2
  GU19: Light 1A 2
South Hill GU1: Guild 5D 38 (6F 23)
South Rd. GU2: Guild 2D 22
  GU21: Wok 6E 4
  GU24: Bisl 7F 3
South St. GU7: G'mng 3K 33
  (not continuous)
South Vw. Ct. GU22: Wok 2G 11
Southway GU21: Guild 3C 22
Southway Ct. GU2: Guild 4A 22
Southwood Av. GU21: Knap 2K 9
Southwood Chase GU6: Cranl 7F 36
Soyer Ct. GU21: Wok 2A 10
Sparvell Rd. GU21: Wok 3H 9
Spectrum
  (Park & Ride) 2H 23
Spectrum Leisure Complex 3G 23
Speedwell Cl. GU4: Guild 1A 24
Spence Av. KT14: Byfl 5J 7
Spencer Ct. GU1: Guild 4A 6
Spiceall GU3: Comp 4H 27
Spike, The 6H 23
  (off Warren Rd.)
Spinney, The GU2: Guild 3C 22
  GU23: Send 4G 19
Spring Cl. GU7: G'mng 6A 28
Spring Ct. GU2: Guild 7D 16
Springfield GU18: Light 2D 2
Springfield Cl. GU21: Knap 2A 10
Springfield Rd.
  GU1: Guild 3E 38 (5G 23)
Springflower Cotts. GU3: Worp . . .1J 21
Spring Gro. GU7: G'mng 6A 28
Springhaven Cl. GU1: Guild 4J 23
Springside Cl. GU1: Guild 3E 22
Springwood GU8: Mil 6G 33
Spruce Dr. GU18: Light 3A 2
Spur, The GU21: Knap 2K 9
Square, The GU2: Guild 6B 22
  GU18: Light 1C 2
  GU23: Wis 7J 7
Squirrel Keep KT14: W Byf 3J 7
Squirrel's Cl. GU7: G'mng 5K 27
Squirrel Wood KT14: W Byf 3J 7
Stable Cotts. GU7: G'mng 7C 28
Stables, The GU1: Guild 1F 23
Staff Cotts. GU7: G'mng 7J 33
STAFFORDLAKE 2F 9
Stafford Lake GU24: Bisl 2F 9
  GU24: Bisl 2F 9

Stag Hill GU2: Guild 5C 22
Stag Hill Ct. GU2: Guild 4D 22
Stainton Wlk. GU21: Wok 2E 10
Stakescorner Rd. GU3: Art 5C 28
Stamford Ho. GU24: Chob 2A 4
  (off Bagshot Rd.)
STANFORD COMMON 3E 14
Stanford Cotts. GU24: Pirb 3E 14
Staniland Dr. KT13: Weyb 2K 7
Stanley Hill GU24: Pirb 6C 8
Stanley Rd. GU21: Wok 7H 5
Stanton Cl. GU6: Cranl 5A 36
Stantons Wharf GU5: Bram 7J 29
Staple La. GU4: E Clan 2H 25
Star Cl. GU5: Shere 4K 25
Starwood Cl. KT14: W Byf 2G 7
Station App.
  GU1: Guild 3E 38 (5G 23)
  GU3: Flex 4B 20
  GU4: Shalf 3G 29
  GU7: G'mng 3K 33
  GU22: Wok 2H 11
  KT14: W Byf 6G 6
Station La. GU8: Ent G, Mil 6G 33
Station Pl. GU7: G'mng 7B 28
Station Rd. GU4: Shalf 3G 29
  GU5: Bram 1H 35
  GU7: G'mng 7B 28
  (Grays Rd.)
  GU7: G'mng 3K 33
  (Station App.)
  GU24: Chob 2B 4
  KT14: W Byf 3E 6
Station Row GU4: Shalf 3G 29
Station Vw. GU1: Guild 3A 38 (5E 22)
Staveley Way GU21: Knap 1A 10
Stepbridge Path GU21: Wok 1F 11
Stephenson Rd. GU2: Guild 4K 21
Stewart Cl. GU21: Wok 1B 10
Stile Ho. GU4: Guild 3B 24
  (off Merrow St.)
Stirling Rd. GU2: Guild 4K 21
Stockers La. GU22: Wok 4H 11
  (not continuous)
Stockland Sq. GU6: Cranl 5B 36
Stocton Cl. GU1: Guild 1B 38 (3E 22)
Stocton Rd. GU1: Guild 1B 38 (3F 23)
Stoke Flds. GU1: Guild 3C 38 (4F 23)
Stoke Gro. GU1: Guild 2D 38 (4F 23)
Stoke Hospital GU1: Guild 2D 38
Stoke M. GU1: Guild 3D 38 (5F 23)
Stoke Mill Cl. GU1: Guild 2F 23
Stoke Pk.
  Guildford 3G 23
Stoke Pk. Ct.
  GU1: Guild 2D 38 (4F 23)
Stoke Rd. GU1: Guild 1D 38 (3F 23)
Stoke Sq. GU1: Guild 2C 38
Stonebridge Flds. GU4: Shalf 4F 29
Stonebridge Wharf GU4: Shalf 4F 29
Stonecrop Rd. GU4: Guild 2A 24
Stonehill Rd. GU18: Light 1A 2
  GU24: Chob 1E 4
Stonepit Cl. GU7: G'mng 3H 33
Stooney Brook GU2: Guild 3A 22
Stoop Ct. KT14: W Byf 3F 7
Storr's La. GU3: Worp 1J 15
Stoughton Rd. GU1: Guild 1C 22
  GU2: Guild 1C 22
Strathavon Cl. GU6: Cranl 1A 36
Strathcona Gdns. GU21: Knap 2K 9
  (not continuous)
Stratton Cl. GU2: Guild 2C 22
Strawberry Cl. GU24: Brkwd 5D 8
Strawberry Flds. GU24: Bisl 6G 3
Strawberry Ri. GU24: Bisl 6G 3
Stream Banks GU3: Woo V 3H 21
Stream Cl. KT14: Byfl 3H 7
Street, The GU3: Comp 3G 27
  GU3: Putt 2B 26
  GU4: E Clan 1H 25
  GU4: Shalf 2F 29
  GU4: W Cla 5E 18
  GU5: Alb 2F 31
  GU5: Wone 7J 29
  GU6: Ewh 2K 37
  (not continuous)
  GU8: Shack 6C 26
Streeters Cl. GU7: G'mng 1C 34
Streets Heath GU24: W End 3F 3
Stringer's Av. GU4: Jac W 5F 17
STRINGERS COMMON 6E 16
Stringhams Copse GU23: Rip 1D 18
Struan Gdns. GU21: Wok 6G 5
Strudwicks Fld. GU6: Cranl 4E 36
Stuart Ct. GU7: G'mng 3A 34
Studland Rd. KT14: W Byf 4K 7
Sturt Ct. GU4: Guild 2K 23
Suffield La. GU3: Putt 5A 26

Suffolk Dr. GU4: Burp 6K 17
Summer Cl. KT14: Byfl 5K 7
Summerhayes Cl. GU21: Wok 5G 5
Summerhill GU7: G'mng 1K 33
Summerhouse Cl.
  GU7: G'mng 4K 33
Summerhouse Rd.
  GU7: G'mng 4K 33
Summerlands GU6: Cranl 4D 36
Summersbury Dr. GU4: Shalf 5G 29
Summersbury Hall GU4: Shalf 5G 29
Summersby Cl. GU7: G'mng 7B 28
Summers Cl. KT13: Weyb 2K 7
Summers La. GU7: Hurt 6G 27
Summer's Rd. GU7: G'mng 7B 28
Sundew Cl. GU18: Light 2D 2
Sundridge Rd. GU22: Wok 3J 11
Sun Hill GU22: Wok 5C 10
Sunnyside GU21: Knap 3H 9
Surrey Cloisters GU7: G'mng 1B 34
Surrey County Cricket Cen. 2J 23
Surrey Ct. GU2: Guild 4D 22
Surrey Gild Craft Gallery 7E 32
Surrey Hills Pk. GU3: Norm 1E 26
Surrey History Cen. 2F 11
Surrey Research Pk., The
  . . . . .4K 21
Surrey Sports Pk. 4C 22
Surrey Technology Cen.
  GU2: Guild 5K 21
Surrey Way GU2: Guild 3D 22
Sussex Cl. GU21: Knap 2J 9
Sussex Ct. GU21: Knap 2J 9
Sussex Pl. GU21: Knap 2J 9
Sussex Rd. GU21: Knap 2J 9
Sutherland Av. GU4: Jac W 5G 17
Sutherland Dr. GU4: Burp 1H 23
Sutton Cl. GU21: Wok 3A 10
SUTTON GREEN 3H 17
Sutton Grn. Rd. GU4: Sut G 3G 17
Sutton Hill GU4: Burp 6A 18
Sutton Lodge GU1: Guild 4G 23
  (off Clandon Rd.)
SUTTON PARK 3H 17
Swallow Cl. GU6: Cranl 4F 37
Swallow Ri. GU21: Knap 1J 9
Swan Cl. GU1: Guild 2F 23
Swan La. GU1: Guild 4C 38 (5F 23)
Swayne's La. GU1: Guild 4C 24
Sycamore Av. GU7: G'mng 7J 33
  GU22: Wok 4G 11
Sycamore Ct. GU1: Guild 5G 23
  (off Harvey Rd.)
  GU7: G'mng 6B 28
Sycamore Rd.
  GU1: Guild 1C 38 (4F 23)
Sydenham Rd.
  GU1: Guild 5D 38 (6F 23)
Sydney Pl. GU1: Guild 5H 23
Sydney Rd. GU1: Guild 5H 23
Sylvan Cl. GU22: Wok 1K 11
Sylvaways Cl. GU6: Cranl 5F 37
Sythwood GU21: Wok 1D 10
Szabo Cres. GU3: Flex 4B 20

T

Tamarind Cl. GU2: Guild 6C 16
Tamerton Sq. GU22: Wok 3G 11
Tangier Rd. GU1: Guild 5J 23
Tanglewood Cl. GU22: Pyr 7B 6
Tanglewood Ride GU24: W End . . .3D 2
Tangley La. GU3: Guild 7B 16
Tanner Ho. GU7: G'mng 3A 34
  (off Flambard Way)
Tannersfield GU4: Shalf 5G 29
Tanners M. GU7: G'mng 1B 34
Tannery La. GU5: Bram 6H 29
  GU23: Send 7B 12
Tansy Cl. GU4: Guild 2A 24
Tarragon Cl. GU2: Guild 7C 16
Tarragon Dr. GU2: Guild 6C 16
Tarragon Rd. GU2: Guild 7C 16
Tarragon Way GU7: G'mng 7J 33
Taylors Cres. GU6: Cranl 5E 36
Teale Cl. GU7: G'mng 1B 34
Tegg's La. GU22: Pyr 7D 6
Telford Ct. GU1: Guild 4H 23
Temple Bar Rd. GU21: Wok 3B 10
Templecombe M. GU22: Wok 7K 5
Tenacre GU21: Wok 2C 10
Tenniel Cl. GU2: Guild 2D 22
Terrace, The GU22: Wok 4J 11
  (not continuous)
Testard Rd. GU2: Guild 5A 38 (6E 22)
Teviot Cl. GU2: Guild 1C 22
Tewkesbury Cl. KT14: Byfl 2H 7
Thatchers La. GU3: Worp 4K 15

The . . . . . .
Names prefixed with 'The'
for example 'The Alders' are
indexed under the main name
such as 'Alders, The'
Thistledene KT14: W Byf 4D 6
Thistley La. GU6: Cranl 4D 36
Thompson's Cl. GU24: Pirb 7D 8
Thorley Cl. KT14: W Byf 5E 6
Thorley Gdns. GU22: Pyr 6E 6
Thornash Cl. GU21: Wok 6E 4
Thornash Rd. GU21: Wok 6E 4
Thornash Way GU21: Wok 6E 4
Thorn Bank GU2: Guild 6C 22
Thornberry Rd. GU1: Guild 7H 17
THORNCOMBE STREET 6F 35
Thorncombe St. GU5: Bram 4F 35
Thornton Cl. GU2: Guild 1C 22
Thorpe's Cl. GU2: Guild 1C 22
Thorsden Cl. GU22: Wok 3G 11
Thorsden Ct. GU22: Wok 2G 11
Three Gates GU1: Guild 3A 24
Three Pears Rd. GU1: Guild 4C 24
Threshold Way GU24: Chob 1G 5
Thrift Va. GU1: Guild 1B 24
Thrupp Ho. GU4: Guild 3B 24
                                    (off Merrow St.)
Thurlow Wlk. GU6: Cranl 7D 36
Thurlton Ct. GU21: Wok 7G 5
Thursby Rd. GU21: Wok 2C 10
Thyme Ct. GU4: Burp 1K 23
Tilehouse Rd. GU1: Guild 1G 29
Tillingbourne Rd. GU4: Shalf 3G 29
Tilthams Cnr. Rd. GU5: Bram 6D 28
        GU7: G'mng 6D 28
Tilthams Grn. GU7: G'mng 6D 28
Timber Cl. GU22: Pyr 5D 6
Tintagel Way GU22: Wok 7J 5
Tithebarns La. GU23: Send 3E 18
Tolldene Cl. GU21: Knap 1A 10
Tollgate GU1: Guild 4B 24
Tolvaddon Cl. GU21: Wok 1C 10
Tormead Rd. GU1: Guild 4H 23
Torrens Cl. GU2: Guild 1C 22
Torridon Cl. GU21: Wok 1D 10
Tottenham Rd. GU7: G'mng 1A 34
Tourist Info. Cen.
        Guildford 4D 38 (5F 23)
Tower Cl. GU21: Wok 1F 11
Tower Ho. KT14: Byfl 3J 7
                                     (off High Rd.)
Town End Cl. GU7: G'mng 3A 34
Town End St. GU7: G'mng 3A 34
Townsend La. GU22: Wok 5K 11
Townslow La. GU23: Wis 7G 7
Town Sq. GU21: Wok 1G 11
Tracious Cl. GU21: Wok 7D 4
Tracious La. GU21: Wok 7D 4
Trade City KT14: Weyb 1J 7
Traditions Golf Course 6F 7
Treebys Av. GU4: Jac W 5F 17
Tregarth Pl. GU21: Wok 1B 10
Trelawne Dr. GU6: Cranl 6D 36
Trenance GU21: Wok 1C 10
Trencham Cres. GU22: Wok 5J 11
Tresillian Way GU21: Wok 7C 4
Tresta Wlk. GU21: Wok 7C 4
Trevose Av. KT14: W Byf 5D 6
Triangle, The GU21: Wok 2E 10
Trigg's Cl. GU22: Wok 3F 11
Trigg's La. GU21: Wok 3E 10
        GU22: Wok 3E 10
Tringham Cl. GU21: Knap 2J 9
Tringham Cotts. GU24: W End 3F 3
Trinity Chyd.
        GU1: Guild 5D 38 (6F 23)
Trinity Ga. GU1: Guild 4E 38
Trinity Rd. GU21: Knap 2H 9
Trodd's La. GU1: Guild 3B 24
        GU4: Guild 3B 24
Trotters La. GU24: Chob 3D 4
Trunley Heath Rd. GU5: Bram 7E 28
Tuckers Cnr. GU6: Cranl 5A 36
Tuckers Dr. GU6: Cranl 5A 36
Tuckey Gro. GU23: Rip 7D 12
Tudor Circ. GU7: G'mng 7A 28
Tudor Cl. GU22: Wok 1J 11
Tudor Ct. GU21: Knap 1K 9
Tudor Rd. GU7: G'mng 7A 28
Tudor Way GU21: Knap 3J 9
TUESLEY 6J 33
Tuesley Cnr. GU7: G'mng 4K 33
Tuesley La. GU7: G'mng 4K 33
Tunsgate GU1: Guild 5D 38 (6F 23)
Tunsgate Sq. GU1: Guild 5C 38
Turfhouse La. GU24: Chob 1A 4
Turner Cl. GU4: Burp 1H 23
Turnoak Av. GU22: Wok 4G 11
Turnoak La. GU22: Wok 4G 11

Turnville Cl. GU18: Light 1A 2
Twycross Rd. GU7: G'mng 7K 27
Twyford Ct. GU1: Guild 4C 22
Tychbourne Dr. GU4: Guild 1A 24
Tylehost GU2: Guild 7C 16
Tylers Ct. GU6: Cranl 5C 36
                                  (off Rowland Rd.)
Tynley Gro. GU4: Jac W 5F 17
Tyrrells Pl. GU1: Guild 5H 23
Tyrwhitt Ct. GU2: Guild 7D 16
                                   (off Grange Rd.)
Tythebarn Cl. GU4: Burp 6K 17
Tyting Cotts. GU4: Guild 7A 24

U

Ullswater Cl. GU18: Light 1B 2
Ullswater Rd. GU18: Light 1B 2
Ulwin Av. KT14: Byfl 4J 7
Underhill Cl. GU7: G'mng 4A 34
Union St. GU24: Brkwd 5A 8
University Ct.
        GU2: Guild 2A 38 (4D 22)
University of Surrey
        Austin Pearce Building
        . . . . .2A 38 (4C 22)
Unstead La. GU5: Bram 7E 28
Unstead Wood GU3: Peasm 5E 28
UNSTED 2F 35
Upfold Cl. GU6: Cranl 2A 36
Upfold La. GU6: Cranl 3A 36
Upfolds Grn. GU4: Burp 1K 23
Uplands Rd. GU1: Guild 4K 23
UPPER EASHING 3G 33
Up. Edgeborough Rd.
        GU1: Guild 5H 23
Up. Guildown Rd.
        GU2: Guild 7A 38 (7D 22)
Up. Manor Rd. GU7: G'mng 7A 28
        GU8: Mil 6E 32
Up. Queen St. GU7: G'mng 3A 34
Upper Stanford GU24: Pirb 2F 15
Upper St. GU5: Shere 1K 31
Upperton Rd.
        GU2: Guild 5A 38 (5E 22)
Upshot La. GU22: Pyr 1D 12
Upton GU21: Wok 1D 10
Urnfield Cl. GU1: Guild 4K 23

V

Vale Cl. GU21: Wok 7G 5
Va. Farm Rd. GU21: Wok 1G 11
Vale Ho. GU21: Wok 1G 11
Valley, The GU2: Guild 1E 28
Valley Vw. GU7: G'mng 3K 33
Vanners Pde. KT14: Byfl 4J 7
Vantage Ct. GU21: Wok 1F 11
Vapery La. GU24: Pirb 5D 8
Vaughan Ct. GU22: Guild 7D 12
                                   (off Grange Rd.)
Venton Cl. GU21: Wok 1D 10
Verites GU7: G'mng 7J 27
Vernon Way GU2: Guild 3B 22
Verralls GU22: Wok 1K 11
                                    (not continuous)
Veryan GU21: Wok 1C 10
Viburnum Ct. GU24: W End 4E 2
Vicarage Ga. GU2: Guild 6C 22
Vicarage La. GU23: Send 3A 18
Vicarage Rd. GU22: Wok 5H 11
        GU24: Chob 2K 3
Vicarage Wlk. GU7: G'mng 2K 33
                                  (off Borough Rd.)
Vickers Dr. Nth. KT13: Weyb 1J 7
Vickers Dr. Sth. KT13: Weyb 2J 7
Victoria Pl. GU21: Wok 7J 5
                                   (off North Rd.)
Victoria Way GU1: Guild . . .2E 38 (4G 23)
        GU6: Cranl 5C 36
        GU7: G'mng 3A 34
        GU21: Knap 1K 9
        GU22: Wok 1G 11
Viggory La. GU21: Wok 6E 4
Village, The GU6: Ewh 2J 37
Village Way GU6: Cranl 5C 36
Vine Cl. GU3: Worp 3K 15
Vine Cotts. GU6: Cranl 5A 36
Virgin Active
        Guildford 7D 16
Viscount Gdns. KT14: Byfl 3J 7

W

Waggon Cl. GU2: Guild 3A 22
Wake Cl. GU2: Guild 6D 16

Wake Ct. GU2: Guild 1D 22
Wakefield Cl. KT14: Byfl 3J 7
Wakehurst Path GU21: Wok 5A 6
Walden Cotts. GU21: Norm 2A 20
Waldens Pk. Rd. GU21: Wok 7E 4
Waldens Rd. GU21: Wok 1F 11
Waldy Ri. GU6: Cranl 4D 36
Wallace Ct. GU3: Worp 1J 21
Walnut Tree Cl.
        GU1: Guild 1A 38 (4E 22)
Walnut Tree Gdns. GU7: G'mng 7A 28
Walnut Tree La. KT14: Byfl 3H 7
Walnut Tree Pk.
        GU1: Guild 1A 38 (4E 22)
Walnut Tree Pl. GU23: Send 1E 18
Walsham M. GU23: Rip 5G 13
Waltham Av. GU2: Guild 7D 16
Walton Av. GU21: Wok 7J 5
Walton Rd. GU21: Wok 6K 5
Walton Ter. GU21: Wok 6K 5
WANBOROUGH 7C 20
Wanborough Bus. Cen.
        GU3: Flex 5E 20
WANBOROUGH COMMON 3F 27
Wanborough Great Barn 7C 20
Wanborough Hill GU3: Wanb 7C 20
Wanborough La. GU6: Cranl 4F 37
Wanborough Station (Rail) 4C 20
Wansford Grn. GU21: Wok 1B 10
Warbury La. GU21: Knap 6H 3
Ward St. GU1: Guild 4D 38 (5F 23)
Warners La. GU5: Alb 4J 31
Warramill Rd. GU7: G'mng 2C 34
Warren Farm Mobile Home Pk.
        GU22: Pyr 7C 6
Warrenhyrst GU1: Guild 5J 23
Warren La. GU5: Alb 2G 31
        GU22: Pyr 2E 12
Warren Rd. GU1: Guild 5H 23
        GU7: G'mng 7A 28
        KT15: New H 1E 6
Warwick La. GU21: Wok 3C 10
Warwicks Bench
        GU1: Guild 6D 38 (6F 23)
Warwick's Bench La.
        GU1: Guild 7H 23
Warwick's Bench Rd.
        GU1: Guild 7E 38 (7G 23)
Waterbrook Pl. GU7: G'mng 2B 34
Watercress Way GU21: Wok 1D 10
Waterden Cl. GU1: Guild 5H 23
Waterden Rd. GU1: Guild 5G 23
Waterers Ri. GU21: Knap 1K 9
Water La. GU5: Alb 1F 31
        GU2: Bisl 3E 8
Watermead GU21: Wok 7B 4
Waterperry La. GU24: Chob 1A 4
Watersedge Dr. GU7: G'mng 2B 34
                                  (off Alderbank Dr.)
Waterside Cen., The 2F 23
Waterside Ct. GU7: G'mng 2C 34
Waterside La. GU7: G'mng 4J 33
Waterside M. GU1: Guild 2E 22
Waterside Rd. GU1: Guild 1F 23
Waterside Way GU21: Wok 2F 11
Watersmeet Cl. GU4: Burp 6J 17
Watery La. GU24: Chob 1A 4
Watford Cl. GU1: Guild 4H 23
Watts Chapel 3H 27
Watts Farm Pde. GU24: Chob 1B 4
                                     (off Barnmead)
Watts Gallery 2H 27
Watts Lea GU21: Wok 6C 4
Waverleigh Rd. GU6: Cranl 7D 36
Waverley Cl. GU22: Wok 2G 11
Wayside Cl. GU21: Wok 7A 4
Weald Cl. GU4: Shalf 3G 29
Wealdon Cl. GU2: Guild 4B 22
Weasdale Cl. GU21: Wok 1B 10
Weatherill Cl. GU1: Guild 4K 23
Webster Ct. GU5: Bram 7H 29
                                  (off Horsham Rd.)
Websters Cl. GU22: Wok 4D 10
Wellirview Pl. GU7: G'mng 2C 34
Well Cl. GU21: Wok 1E 10
Wellington Ter. GU21: Knap 2A 10
Wellington Way KT13: Weyb 1K 7
Well La. GU21: Wok 1E 10
Well Path GU21: Wok 1E 10
Wells La. GU3: Norm 1A 20
Wells Rd. GU1: Guild 1A 24
Wellwynds Rd. GU6: Cranl 6D 36
Wendela Cl. GU22: Wok 2H 11
Wendley Dr. KT15: New H 1E 6
Wendron Cl. GU21: Wok 2C 10
Wendy Cres. GU2: Guild 2C 22
Wentworth Cl. GU23: Rip 5F 13
Wesco Ct. GU21: Wok 1C 10
WESTBOROUGH 3B 22
WESTBROOK 2J 33

Westbrook Rd. GU7: G'mng 2J 33
WEST BYFLEET 4E 6
West Byfleet Golf Course 4D 6
West Byfleet Station (Rail) 3E 6
WEST CLANDON 6E 18
West Ct. GU4: Burp 7K 17
Westdene Mdws. GU6: Cranl 5A 36
West Dr. KT15: New H 1F 7
WEST END 3F 3
Westerfields Cl. GU22: Wok 1A 12
Westermain KT15: New H 1G 7
WESTFIELD 5G 11
Westfield Av. GU22: Wok 5G 11
Westfield Cl. GU22: Wok 5H 11
Westfield Comn. GU22: Wok 6G 11
Westfield Gro. GU22: Wok 4G 11
Westfield Pde. KT15: New H 1H 7
Westfield Rd. GU1: Guild 7G 17
        GU22: Wok 6F 11
Westfield Sq. GU22: Wok 6G 11
Westfield Way GU22: Wok 6G 11
W. Flexford La.
        GU3: Flex, Wanb 4C 20
West Hall KT14: W Byf 4H 7
West Heath GU24: Pirb 7D 8
W. Hill Cl. GU24: Brkwd 4H 9
West Hill Golf Course 4H 9
W. Hill Rd. GU22: Wok 3F 11
West Ho. GU6: Cranl 3B 36
Westmead GU21: Wok 1D 10
West Meads GU2: Guild 5B 22
Westminster Ct.
        GU1: Guild 4E 38 (5G 23)
        GU22: Wok 5K 11
West Mt. GU1: Guild 6A 38 (6E 22)
                                    (not continuous)
Weston Cl. GU7: G'mng 1A 34
Weston Ct. GU7: G'mng 1A 34
Weston Farm Cotts. GU5: Alb 2F 31
Westonfields GU5: Alb 2G 31
Weston Gdns. GU22: Pyr 7C 6
Weston Rd. GU2: Guild 3C 22
                                    (not continuous)
Weston Way GU22: Pyr 7C 6
Weston Yd. GU5: Alb 2G 31
Westside Ct. GU24: W End 4E 2
West St. GU1: Guild 1H 11
Westview GU22: Wok 4F 11
                                     (off Park Dr.)
Westward Ho GU1: Guild 2H 23
Westway GU2: Guild 2B 22
Westwood Av. KT15: Wdhm 3D 6
Westwood Ct. GU2: Guild 3B 22
Westwood La.
        GU3: Flex, Norm, Wanb 2A 20
Wexfenne Gdns. GU22: Pyr 7F 7
Wey and Arun Junction Canal
        Bramley 3K 35
Weybank GU23: Wis 7J 7
Wey Barton KT14: Byfl 4K 7
Weybourne Way KT15: New H 1G 7
Weybrook Dr. GU4: Burp 6K 17
Wey Cl. KT14: W Byf 4F 7
Wey Ct. GU1: Guild 3B 38 (5E 22)
        GU7: G'mng 1C 34
        GU22: Wok 3G 11
                                  (off Claremont Av.)
Wey Ct. Cl. GU7: G'mng 1B 34
Weydown Cl. GU2: Guild 6C 16
Weydown La. GU2: Guild 6C 16
Weylea Av. GU4: Burp 1J 23
Weymede KT14: Byfl 3K 7
Wey Retail Pk. KT14: Byfl 3J 7
Wey Rd. GU7: G'mng 2C 34
Weyside Cl. KT14: Byfl 3K 7
Weyside Gdns. GU1: Guild 2E 22
Weyside Pl. GU7: G'mng 2C 34
Weyside Rd. GU1: Guild 2D 22
Weyvern Pk. GU3: Peasm 5D 28
Weyvern Pl. GU3: Peasm 5D 28
Weyview Cl. GU1: Guild 2E 22
Wey Vw. Ct. GU1: Guild 3A 38 (5E 22)
Weyview Gdns. GU7: G'mng 2B 34
Wharf, The GU7: G'mng 2B 34
Wharf La. GU23: Rip 2H 13
        GU23: Send 2A 12
Wharf Rd. GU1: Guild 2B 38 (4E 22)
Wharf St. GU7: G'mng 3A 34
Whateley Cl. GU2: Guild 6D 16
Wheatsheaf Cl. GU21: Wok 7G 5
Wherwell Rd.
        GU2: Guild 5A 38 (6E 22)
Whipley Cl. GU4: Burp 6K 17
White Ct. GU2: Guild 1C 22
White Ga. GU22: Wok 4H 11
White Hart Cl. GU23: Rip 5G 13
White Hart La. GU3: Woo V 3G 21
White Hart Mdws. GU23: Rip 5G 13
White Horse La. GU23: Rip 5G 13

White Ho. Dr. GU1: Guild 4K 23
White Ho. La. GU4: Jac W 6F 17
White La. GU4: Guild 6A 24
  GU5: Alb 6A 24
White Lion Wlk.
  GU1: Guild 5C 38 (5F 23)
Whitemore Rd. GU1: Guild 7F 17
White Pillars GU22: Wok 4D 10
White Rose La. GU22: Wok 2H 11
White Rose Lane Local Nature Reserve
  ......3K 11
Whites La. GU24: Pirb 1G 15
White Star Cl. GU7: G'mng 7B 28
Whitethorn Cotts. GU6: Cranl ..3A 36
Whitfield Cl. GU21: Wok 1C 22
Whitmoor & Rickford Commons
  Local Nature Reserve 4C 16
WHITMOOR COMMON 3C 16
Whitmoor La. GU4: Sut G 3F 17
Whopshott Av. GU21: Wok 7E 4
Whopshott Cl. GU21: Wok 7E 4
Whopshott Dr. GU21: Wok 7E 4
Wiggins Yd. GU7: G'mng 3A 34
Wilbury Rd. GU21: Wok 1F 11
Wilcot Cl. GU24: Bisl 7G 3
Wilcot Gdns. GU24: Bisl 7G 3
Wildacres KT14: W Byf 2H 7
Wildbank Ct. GU22: Wok 2H 11
Wilderness Cl. GU22: Guild 6B 22
Wilderness Rd. GU2: Guild 6B 22
Wilders Cl. GU21: Wok 2E 10
Wildfield Cl. GU3: Woo V 3H 21
Wildwood Cl. GU6: Cranl 7E 36
  GU22: Pyr 6D 6
Wilfred St. GU21: Wok 1G 11
WILLEY GREEN 1D 20
William St. GU1: Guild 2B 38 (4E 22)
William Russell Ct. GU21: Wok ..2A 10
Williams Pl. GU6: Ewh 3K 37
William's Wlk. GU21: Wok 7D 16
Willow Bank GU22: Wok 6G 11
Willow Cl. GU6: Cranl 7E 36
  KT15: Wdhm 2D 6
Willow Dr. GU3: Flex 4C 20
  GU23: Rip 1E 18
Willow Grn. GU24: W End 4F 3
Willow La. GU1: Guild 3J 23
Willowmead Cl. GU21: Wok 7C 4
Willow Rd. GU7: G'mng 6B 28
Willows, The GU2: Guild 6C 16
  (off Weydown La.)
  GU4: Guild 2A 24
  GU18: Light 2C 2
  KT14: Byfl 4J 7
Willows Pk. GU3: Norm 1D 20
Willow Wlk. GU5: Shere 2K 31
Willow Way GU1: Guild 7D 16
  GU22: Wok 5G 11
  KT14: W Byf 2G 7
Wilson Way GU21: Wok 7F 5
Windermere Ct. GU21: Wok 2C 10
  (off St John's Rd.)
Windermere Rd. GU18: Light ...1B 2

Windgates GU4: Guild 1A 24
Windlemere Golf Course 2E 2
Windlesham Rd. GU24: W End ..2E 2
Windrush Cl. GU5: Bram 1H 35
Windsor Cl. GU22: Guild 6B 22
  GU7: G'mng 3A 34
Windsor Ct. GU24: Chob 1A 4
Windsor Ct. Rd. GU24: Chob ...1A 4
Windsor Rd. GU24: Chob 1A 4
Windsor Way GU22: Wok 7A 6
Winds Ridge GU23: Send 2A 18
Windy Wood GU7: G'mng 4J 33
Winern Glebe KT14: Byfl 4H 7
Wingfield Cl. KT15: New H 1F 7
Winnards GU21: Wok 2C 10
Winnington Way GU21: Wok ...2D 10
Winston Churchill School Sports Cen.
  ......2A 10
Winston Way GU21: Wok 4K 11
Winterhill Way GU4: Burp 7K 17
Wintersells Ind. Est. KT14: Byfl ..1J 7
Wintersells Rd. KT14: Byfl 1H 7
Wishbone Way GU21: Wok 7B 4
WISLEY 7J 7
Wisley Golf Course 1H 13
Wisley La. GU23: Wis 7G 7
Withies, The GU21: Knap 1A 10
Withies La. GU3: Comp 4J 27
Withy Cl. GU18: Light 1C 2
Wodeland Av.
  GU2: Guild 6A 38 (6D 22)
WOKING 1H 11
Woking Bus. Pk. GU21: Wok ...6K 5
WOKING COMMUNITY HOSPITAL
  ......2H 11
Woking Crematorium
  GU21: Wok 3A 10
Woking FC 4H 11
Woking Golf Course 4C 10
WOKING HOSPICE 2H 11
  (off High View Road)
Woking Leisure Cen. 3H 11
WOKING NUFFIELD HEALTH HOSPITAL
  ......5G 5
WOKING PRIORY HOSPITAL ...7J 3
Woking Rd. GU1: Guild 7F 17
  (not continuous)
  GU4: Jac W 5E 16
Woking Station (Rail) 1H 11
Wolesley Ct. GU21: Knap 2J 9
  (off Tudor Way)
Wolseley Rd. GU7: G'mng 1A 34
Wolsey Pl. Shop. Cen.
  GU21: Wok 1G 11
Wolsey Wlk. GU21: Wok 1G 11
WONERSH 7K 29
WONERSH COMMON 5K 29
Wonersh Comn. Rd.
  GU5: Wone 5K 29
Wonersh Pk. GU5: Wone 1K 35
Woodbridge Bus. Pk.
  GU1: Guild 3E 22
WOODBRIDGE HILL 3D 22

Woodbridge Hill GU2: Guild 3D 22
Woodbridge Hill Gdns.
  GU2: Guild 3C 22
Woodbridge Mdws.
  GU1: Guild 1A 38, 1A 38 (3E 22)
Woodbridge Rd.
  GU1: Guild 1B 38 (3E 22)
Woodbridge Trade & Retail Pk.
  GU1: Guild 1A 38
Woodcote GU2: Guild 1D 28
  GU6: Cranl 4A 36
  GU7: G'mng 1K 33
Wood Cl. GU21: Wok 2D 22
Woodend Cl. GU21: Wok 3C 10
Woodger Cl. GU4: Guild 2C 10
WOODHAM 2D 6
Woodham Ga. GU21: Wok 4A 6
Woodham Hall Est. GU21: Wok ..5K 5
Woodham La. GU21: Wok 5K 5
  KT15: Wdhm, New H 3C 6
Woodham Lock KT14: W Byf ...3D 6
Woodham Pk. Rd. KT15: Wdhm ..1D 6
Woodham Pk. Way KT15: Wdhm ..2D 6
Woodham Pl. GU21: Wok 5H 5
Woodham Ri. GU21: Wok 5H 5
Woodham Rd. GU21: Wok 6G 5
Woodham Waye GU21: Wok 4K 5
Woodhill GU23: Send 3B 18
Woodhill Ct. GU23: Send 2B 18
Woodland Av. GU6: Cranl 5E 36
Woodland Cl. GU7: G'mng 2B 34
Woodlands GU22: Wok 2H 11
  GU23: Send 2D 18
Woodlands, The GU1: Guild 3A 24
Woodlands Av. KT14: W Byf ...4D 6
Woodlands Cl. GU21: Wok 2C 10
  KT16: Ott 1K 5
  GU22: Wok 3G 11
Woodlands Ho. GU21: Wok 5A 6
Woodlands Pk. GU21: Wok 3K 23
  GU21: Wok 5A 6
Woodlands Rd. GU1: Guild 7F 17
  KT14: W Byf 5D 6
Woodland Vw. GU7: G'mng 5A 28
Wood La. GU21: Knap 2K 9
Woodlawn Gro. GU21: Wok 6H 5
Woodley Ho. GU7: G'mng 6A 28
Woodmancote Gdns.
  KT14: W Byf 4E 6
Woodmancourt GU7: G'mng 6J 27
Woodpecker Way GU22: Wok ...1F 17
Wood Riding GU22: Pyr 6C 6
Wood Ri. GU3: Guild 2A 22
Wood Rd. GU7: G'mng 7B 28
Woodrough Copse GU5: Bram ..2J 35
Woodrough La. GU5: Bram 1H 35
  (off High St.)
Woodruff Av. GU1: Guild 1J 23
Woodside Cl. GU21: Knap 1K 9
Woodside Pk. Ind. Est.
  GU7: G'mng 3B 34

Woodside Rd. GU2: Guild 3B 22
Woodstock GU4: W Cla 5F 19
Woodstock Cl. GU6: Cranl 7E 36
  GU21: Wok 7G 5
Woodstock Gro. GU7: G'mng ...7K 27
Wood St. Grn. GU3: Woo V 2G 21
WOOD STREET VILLAGE 2H 21
Woodway GU1: Guild 3K 23
Woodyers Cl. GU5: Wone 7K 29
Woolsack Ct. GU2: Guild 1C 22
Woolsack Way GU7: G'mng 3A 34
Wootton Grange GU22: Wok ...3G 11
  (off Langley Wlk.)
Worcester Rd. GU2: Guild 2B 22
Workshop Gym
  Guildford 3F 23
WORPLESDON 4A 16
Worplesdon Golf Course 6A 10
Worplesdon Hill GU22: Wok 6J 9
Worplesdon Hill Ho.
  GU22: Wok 6K 9
Worplesdon Rd. GU2: Guild ...5A 16
  GU3: Guild, Worp 2J 15
Worplesdon Station (Rail) 1D 16
Worsfold Cl. GU23: Send 7K 11
Wyatts Almshouses
  GU7: G'mng 1C 34
  (off Wyatt's Cl.)
Wyatt's Cl. GU7: G'mng 1C 34
Wych Elm Ri. GU1: Guild 7G 23
Wychelm Rd. GU18: Light 2C 2
Wych Hill GU22: Wok 3E 10
Wych Hill La. GU22: Wok 3F 11
Wych Hill Pk. GU22: Wok 3F 11
Wych Hill Ri. GU22: Wok 3E 10
Wych Hill Way GU22: Wok 4F 11
Wycliffe Bldgs. GU2: Guild 5B 38
WYKE 2A 20
Wyke Cross GU3: Norm 2A 20
Wykeham Rd. GU1: Guild 3B 24
Wykehurst La. GU6: Ewh 2G 37
Wyndham Cres. GU6: Cranl ...5A 36
Wyndham Rd. GU21: Wok 2D 10
Wyphurst Rd. GU6: Cranl 4C 37

Y

Yellowcress Dr. GU24: Bisl 7G 3
Yews, The KT14: Byfl 3J 7
Yew Tree Dr. GU1: Guild 7E 16
York Cl. KT14: Byfl 3J 7
York Rd. GU1: Guild 3C 38 (3J 23)
  GU22: Wok 3F 11
  KT14: Byfl 3J 7
Youngstroat La. GU24: Chob ...1G 5
Yvonne Arnaud Theatre
  Guildford 5C 38 (6F 23)

Z

Zinnia Dr. GU24: Bisl 7G 3

MIX
Paper from responsible sources
FSC® C004309
www.fsc.org

SAFETY CAMERA INFORMATION

PocketGPSWorld.com's CamerAlert is a self-contained speed and red light camera warning system for SatNavs and Android or Apple iOS smartphones/tablets. Visit www.cameralert.com to download.

Safety camera locations are publicised by the Safer Roads Partnership which operates them in order to encourage drivers to comply with speed limits at these sites. It is the driver's absolute responsibility to be aware of and to adhere to speed limits at all times.

By showing this safety camera information it is the intention of Geographers' A-Z Map Company Ltd. to encourage safe driving and greater awareness of speed limits and vehicle speed. Data accurate at time of printing.